NO RETREAT, NO SURRENDER

NO RETREAT, NO SURRENDER

ONE AMERICAN'S FIGHT

Tom DeLay
with Stephen Mansfield

SENTINEL

SENTINEL
Published by the Penguin Group
Penguin Group (USA) Inc., 375 Hudson Street, New York, New York 10014, U.S.A.
Penguin Group (Canada), 90 Eglinton Avenue East, Suite 700,
Toronto, Ontario, Canada M4P 2Y3 (a division of Pearson Penguin Canada Inc.)
Penguin Books Ltd, 80 Strand, London WC2R 0RL, England
Penguin Ireland, 25 St. Stephen's Green, Dublin 2, Ireland
(a division of Penguin Books Ltd)
Penguin Books Australia Ltd, 250 Camberwell Road, Camberwell, Victoria 3124, Australia
(a division of Pearson Australia Group Pty Ltd)
Penguin Books India Pvt Ltd, 11 Community Centre, Panchsheel Park,
New Delhi – 110 017, India
Penguin Group (NZ), 67 Apollo Drive, Mairangi Bay, Auckland 1311, New Zealand
(a division of Pearson New Zealand Ltd)
Penguin Books (South Africa) (Pty) Ltd, 24 Sturdee Avenue,
Rosebank, Johannesburg 2196, South Africa

Penguin Books Ltd, Registered Offices:
80 Strand, London WC2R 0RL, England

First published in 2007 by Sentinel,
a member of Penguin Group (USA) Inc.

10 9 8 7 6 5 4 3 2 1

ISBN 978-1-59523-034-8

Page 189 constitutes a continuation of this copyright page.

Printed in the United States of America
Set in Bodoni Book
Designed by Daniel Lagin

wo years later, ex-Speaker eLay waits to learn legal fate

uan A. Lozano
Associated Press

OUSTON — Former U.S. se Majority Leader Tom ay — still waiting to learn egal fate since being con- d nearly two years ago for role in a scheme to influ- Texas elections — is pray- or vindication but also pre- ng for the possibility of isonment.

9-23-2012

Tom DeLay

Lay's three-year prison ence has been on hold as case has made its way ugh the appellate process. oth DeLay and his critics, process has been frustrat- slow, due in part to some e appeals court justices in in recusing themselves as as DeLay's successful t to have a judge on the l removed because of Republican comments she .

don't like living under this I. But I'm not angry about ven pray for the prosecu- and my enemies," the er Houston-area congress- said. "No, they have not oyed Tom DeLay as a per-

son. And I'm ready to go to prison if that's where I'm sup- posed to end up."

But DeLay, and his attor- ney, Brian Wice, are hop- ing to get his convictions overturned. On Oct. 10, they will finally get a chance to make their case to the 3rd Court of Appeals, arguing the once-powerful Republican leader did nothing wrong and is the victim of a political ven- detta, a claim that prosecutors deny.

DeLay, 65, was found guilty in November 2010 of money laundering and conspiracy to commit money laundering for helping illegally funnel corpo- rate money to Texas candidates in 2002.

Sitting with DeLay in his office in downtown Houston on Wednesday, Wice used a lit- erary allusion to explain the case. He compared DeLay to Jean Valjean, the kind-hearted

protagonist of Victor Hugo's "Les Misérables." He called Ronnie Earle, the now-retired Democratic Travis County Dis- trict Attorney in Austin who charged the former lawmaker, a modern-day Inspector Javert, who pursued Valjean at all costs.

The Travis County District Attorney's Office says the case was never about politics but about someone who broke Texas law.

"Our office has always been fair and never been politically motivated in prosecuting this defendant or any other," said prosecutor Holly Taylor.

Jurors in Austin determined DeLay conspired with two asso- ciates, John Colyandro and Jim Ellis, to use his Texas-based political action committee to send a check for $190,000 in corporate money to an arm of the Washington-based Republi- can National Committee. The RNC then sent the same amount to seven Texas House candidates. Under state law, corporate money cannot be given directly to political cam- paigns.

To Christine
My love, my mentor, my loyal opposition,
the true conservative in our family

FOREWORD BY RUSH LIMBAUGH

History is a funny thing. It is continuously being created, but it is not fully understood until those who fashion it are long gone. Time demands that the consequences of every action take their toll, and only when this is complete can one really see the impact, whether positive or negative, that remains. Tom DeLay's impact on history is yet to be determined, though I can assure you that contrary to what many may say today his actions and choices have made America a better place.

My first real awareness of DeLay was around 1992, leading up to the election of 1994. He was part of the Newt Gingrich "Back Bench Bunch" that was causing all kinds of hassles for speakers like Tom Foley and Jim Wright, among others. This Bunch led the Republicans in securing the majority in the House of Representatives in 1995, which is really when the fun begins. The Democrats had run Washington and the House for four decades, and they couldn't adjust to being out of power. Power to them is a birthright; they think it's their entitlement. DeLay came in and made it his agenda to play hardball the way the Democrats had always played hardball. The problem was that the Democrats had forgotten how to play.

DeLay has always known that conservatism is probably the epitome of compassion. Conservatives like DeLay look at humanity and see optimism, great potential, and people who can be better than even they know they can be. Democrats look at average Americans with contempt and see people who can't accomplish and who can't overcome the obstacles of life. That mind-set is necessary for Democrats because it paints Americans as "needy," which gives the Democrats a chance to deploy their welfare policies and big-government benefit programs. They end up just keeping people on the bare edge of subsistence, as history has shown.

People like DeLay see the potential for average, ordinary people to become extraordinary beings and do extraordinary things. That is the big threat to Democrats, and it always has been. If you take the very people whom Democrats look down upon, and whom they feel arrogant condescension toward, and you lift them up by teaching them that they have the ability to do great things, then you remove the need for Democrats. DeLay was a huge threat to the entire ideology of liberalism and, as such, to the entire Democratic Party. He had to be cut down to size. He had to be whittled down to something that was a caricature of the stereotype of conservatism, which is a "mean-spirited, racist, sexist, bigoted homophobe."

He was the victim of this along with Newt Gingrich and a number of others. But the thing about DeLay is that it never deterred him. He never tried to make peace with these people by compromising his own principles. He never tried to go to them and say, "Hey! Stop treating me this way!" or "Please let me extend this peace offering." He just kept fighting them. He just kept defeating them. He never gave up on it. He was hell-bent on reforming the House of Representatives in ways both political and ethical, and he became too big a threat, and he was ultimately targeted for destruction.

The one thing I will never understand about Republicans is their need to prove to the country and Democrats that they are not the mean-spirited stereotype that is associated with their party. They even went so far as to pass a law concerning the House Republican leadership—that if any of them are ever indicted, they are to resign immediately. Democrats don't have such a rule. Democrats don't feel the need to show people how wonderfully magnanimous they are. I think the law was part of an ethics movement designed to show that the Republicans were "clean and pure" and were not going to tolerate nonsense and crime in Congress. I don't know why this rule was written, but once it was in place all the Democrats needed was a political hack prosecutor to indict someone on the basis of nothing. When the indictment triggered the Republican rule, DeLay had to go.

So in essence the Republicans gave the Democrats the tool to get rid of DeLay. With campaign finance law as convoluted as it is right now, you can have the grand jury allege a crime in an indictment with no evidence of any crime whatsoever. This is essentially what happened to DeLay. Where is his trial? It's nowhere to be found, because the purpose of his indictment has already been served. He's gone from the House of Representatives.

The liberal attack on DeLay was classic. It was predictable. What was sad to me, though, was that in the end there were very few people willing to stand up for DeLay and try to refute some of the baseless charges that were bandied around about him. I know now that this was not because they didn't believe in DeLay, but because they were just scared for themselves. But isn't that what separates the leaders from the followers? There were so few in the Republican leadership at the time who had his courage, his conviction, and his willingness to be controversial, and this often left him standing alone. History shows that if there's someone out there leading the way, most men will gladly shrink away into the shadows and let the pioneer take the arrows. Knowing this, DeLay still continued to press forward. For him, the cause was greater than the risk.

He was called the "Exterminator," a play on his past career as the founder of a pest-control company, and the "Hammer," both nicknames associated with his ability to enforce party discipline in close votes and supposedly wreak political vengeance on opponents. Liberals tried to portray him as somebody inhuman, heartless, cold, and cruel because they couldn't defeat his ideas. What they had to do was try to discredit his character and besmirch his reputation so that anything Republicans did could be connected to DeLay as equally coldhearted, mean-spirited, and cruel—when the truth was just the opposite.

The Hammer label didn't refer to his character, but simply to his ability to push legislation through. Is that such a bad thing? The Democrats have Hammers. The idea that Tom DeLay is the only guy in Congress who ever whipped the place into shape is absurd. He just wasn't a Democrat doing it. DeLay was great at carrying the water of the House leadership and of the president. He was in charge of the Republican agenda, and he succeeded. This is why the left hated him.

Another confirmation of DeLay's great character is that he accomplished all this without courting media favor. One of the things that I appreciate about DeLay was that he didn't care about what the media thought. His objective was not to make himself look good. He didn't want a great reputation on the basis of "spin." He didn't want Tom DeLay to be defined as whatever the press said about him in flowery ways. He wanted Tom DeLay to be defined by what he got done, by the work he succeeded in moving through Congress as one of the Republican leadership—and that's what he did. And when you do that in a place like Washington, which is run socially and politically by liberals, you're going to become a target. He was running around with a bull's-eye on his back the whole time he was there, and it didn't change him. It didn't scare him off. It didn't discourage him. He kept raising money. He kept doing what he could to see to it that the Republican majority had the greatest shot they could have for as many years as possible.

I remember one time Tom asked me to accompany him to an orientation for the incoming Republican freshmen that was held at the Library of Congress. I couldn't help thinking that evening that when Tom got up to speak, any Democrats who might have snuck in would have received quite a shock. Liberals would have expected him to read those young politicians the riot act and threaten them with dire consequences if they didn't vote his way. To the contrary, he addressed them as though they were not freshmen at all. He treated them as human beings and as co-equals in the House of Representatives. He was motivational, inspirational, and encouraging. He was not demanding, he didn't threaten, and he didn't insist on certain types of behavior. One of the things he did was inform them about the use of the Library of Congress. He said, "This is your intellectual home. Use it to your advantage however you want." I was quite touched by this because he's actually a gentle, encouraging guy. He's sensitive and thoughtful, seeing those freshmen as future movers and shakers and not as the bottom of the barrel.

History continues to be written, but the people writing history today are not Tom DeLay's friends. They treat Tom DeLay as a man of disgrace and humiliation, a man who was run from office by virtue of this indictment and this "corruption." When people who are not yet born grow up, mature, and begin looking back, they will realize the true history of this era: the history of Republicans securing the majority in the House of Representatives for the first time in forty years; what they did with it over the next twelve years; and who really led it. When that young generation looks back with the clarity of years, they will realize who really made the House work, who got the votes and moved conservative policies forward, who stepped out in support of the president's Medicare prescription drug bill that is showing an 80 percent approval rating by participants, who set up the House of Representatives as a place where Republicans would be empowered for a long time, and who blocked Clinton and forced him to compromise on welfare reform and a balanced budget. It was Tom DeLay who did all these things, and future generations will know it in a way that the present generation does not.

They're also going to see that Republicans lost the House precisely when DeLay's influence was on the decline, which is a testament to his influence and leadership. Tom DeLay is a great administrator. He gets things done. He used his power wisely. The liberal attack on DeLay is the epitome of liberal attacks on all successful conservatives. He was very effective, and he was attacked because he was effective. This in no way negates the impact he has had on American politics. History speaks volumes, and it will reveal itself in the years to come. Tom knows this, because only this belief could keep him going through such strong adversity.

I remember once hearing that before Tom graduated from the University of Houston he was expelled from Baylor University, for offenses including vandalism. He was apparently caught painting Baylor's colors—the famed green and gold—on buildings at rival Texas A&M University. In hindsight and in the great scheme of things, the offense seems small. But the same boldness that led Tom to graffiti a wall in the name of team spirit seems evident in his life today. He spent his years in Congress pushing boundaries, raising bars, and leaping obstacles, regardless of opposition and hostility from the other side. And there were more than a few times when Tom, well aware of the risks, chose to walk right up to the walls built by the liberals—walls of oppression and disbelief. Fueled by his passion for the American people, he pulled out his spray paint and tagged those walls with the colors not only of the Republican Party, but of the American flag—colors that represent what living in this country really means.

Call Tom DeLay a vandal, or the "Exterminator," or the "Hammer" if you wish. I call him a hero, and I call him a friend.

PREFACE BY SEAN HANNITY

L iberals believe that America is better off now that Tom DeLay is no
longer a member of the U.S. House of Representatives. But I believe that America would be better off if all 435 members of the House
were just like Tom DeLay: relentless in defense of traditional values,
personal liberty, small government, the unborn, and America's security.
And savvy about politics.

Tom DeLay is a great American. Make no mistake about that. I am
proud to call him a friend and to stand behind him 100 percent as liberals deviously shift their attacks on him from Congress to the judiciary,
forgetting innocent until proven guilty.

You see, the left in this country despises Tom DeLay. They hate him
for his conservative convictions, his faith, and his recognition that there
is evil in the world against which we must remain vigilant. Most of all,
the left hates Tom DeLay because he is effective.

Thanks in good part to DeLay's keen political sense, Republicans
managed to win the House of Representatives in 1994 and hold on to it
for the next five elections—which is no small feat, given historical
trends and the open hostility to Republicans displayed by many in the
media.

DeLay stepped down in June 2006, and five months later Republicans lost the House. This is not a coincidence, in my opinion.

The conservative movement needs the wisdom of Tom DeLay as we gear up for the 2008 presidential election. If we don't correct the mistakes we made in 2006, we will be forced to contend with yet another President Clinton in the White House—and I don't think I could stand that, could you?

Few leaders in the national Republican party have the guts, resolve, and street smarts that Tom DeLay possesses. While he and I may not agree on every personality mentioned in this book, we do share the same conservative vision for America. I admire his tenacity and his bravery. He has had the courage to come on *Hannity and Colmes* even when the liberal bombardment against him was heaviest.

The great thing about Tom DeLay is that he never changes direction. Not when the going gets tough; not ever. Going forward in politics, even though he is not serving in Congress, we can expect him to hold steady, defending everything you and I hold dear. And to the dismay of liberals everywhere, Tom DeLay will remain dazzlingly effective.

CONTENTS

NO RETREAT, NO SURRENDER

INTRODUCTION: OPENING SALVO

There is a memory that has come back to me often throughout my life. It is the scene of an ordeal that occurred when I was only twelve, yet it has become the defining image of both my life and my politics.

Late in 1959 my family was flying home to the United States after some years living in Venezuela. My father had been the general manager for a Tulsa-based oil company, then known as Helmerich & Payne, that serviced contracts throughout South America. This is what had landed us in the rain forests of Venezuela, where I spent many of my early years. But in time it had all become too much, particularly for my mother. There were revolutions and murders. Dead bodies sometimes hung from lampposts in our village square. I even had a near miss with a death squad, and not long afterward my mother understandably insisted that it was time for us to go home. So while my father concluded his business in Venezuela, my mother, my sister, my younger brother, and I flew back to America.

In those days planes flying from Caracas to the United States made fuel stops in Havana, Cuba. This may sound odd. Fidel Castro's revolution had begun on New Year's Day 1959, and it may seem strange that planes filled with Americans would still be landing at Havana's José Martí Airport in the fall of that year. Remember, though, that the world had yet to see who Castro really was. The United States courted him more than we shunned him in the early months of his revolution, his unfolding thugocracy having yet to fully reveal itself. It was not until February 1960 that Castro signed his oil compact with the Soviet Union, and made his true intentions known to the world. Before then he was still a darling of left-wing America. The rest of America hardly took notice. After Richard Nixon met with Castro he dismissed the Cuban leader as "naïve." And Che Guevara, one of the most detestable lizards ever to crawl out from under Leninism's rock, was still a hero of Western radical chic in late 1959. No, the world had yet to learn—or perhaps dare to acknowledge—who Castro really was.

But I was about to.

Our plane landed in Havana at midday. My mother told us to stay in our seats, and that we would soon be taking off again. My brother and sister fell fast asleep quickly. I stayed awake, though, and looked out the window, and saw a handful of men in shabby green uniforms gathering on the tarmac. They each had a rifle slung across one shoulder, and several of them restrained thickly muscled German shepherds on leather leashes. A moment later one of the soldiers stepped into the front of our cabin and ordered all the Americans off the plane.

Even these many years later it is the smells I remember most. As we fifteen or so terrified Americans inched haltingly off the plane, I breathed the lifeless odor of fuel on the runway, stagnant there between the broiling tarmac and the relentless Caribbean sun. Worse was the stench of the soldiers. Probably fresh from the dank jungle and wearing their only sets of clothes, these guerrillas emitted a smell that somehow seemed part of their evil, to my twelve-year-old senses. They did not know that I spoke Spanish and so they did not know that I understood their vulgarity, their snarling insults. Their words and their stench filled me with a sense of wickedness that has never left me.

We were herded into a flat-roofed, dingy building at the end of the tarmac. Thankfully, a slight breeze worked its way through the windows, but the room was thick with the odors of fifteen perspiring bodies, the soldiers' sweaty foulness, and fear. We were kept there for hours, the leering suggestiveness of the soldiers tormenting the women.

But I was tormented by what I saw on my mother's face. She was a strong Texas woman, but on this day her face betrayed first her worry, then her overwhelming anxiety, and finally her terror. That's when she began to cry. This shattered me, and it was there, sitting on that nasty floor watching my mother weep, her husband a thousand miles away, that I met for the first time the suffocating spirit of tyranny. It filled that room in all of its dark hues. The disregard for life. The soul-killing domination. The complete absence of choice. The stinking wet blanket of helplessness. The brute power that obliterates individuality. The constant threat of death.

In George Orwell's prophetic novel *1984*, a character declares, "If you want a picture of the future, imagine a boot stomping on a human face—forever." There is no better description of communism, and I faced its threatening evil that day in Havana.

After more taunting and intimidation, we were eventually allowed back onto our plane, and hours later we landed safely in the United States. I was grateful, but I have never forgotten. The memory has come back to me time and again. Sometimes the scenes fill my mind so powerfully that I can almost smell that tarmac, almost fill my nostrils again with the stench of Castro's henchmen.

The scene came to me, sometimes several times a day, during the years I served on the floor of the U.S. Congress. It has been present every time I faced down some liberal advance, knowing that today's liberalism is an early stage of the same evil I experienced in Havana. This memory stiffened my resolve when I took a difficult stand before a president who had broken his oath of office, or sought to protect the ways of our Founding Fathers against the encroachments of socialist politics. I have been energized by this image as I fought to protect the unborn, defend the right of Israel to exist in the world, or honored the religious faith that has made our nation great. This image is the face of concentrated political evil in our world, and I have given myself to seeing it destroyed wherever it manifests in my beloved America.

On that steamy Havana tarmac in 1959, Fidel Castro did me a favor. He showed me the contorted face of leftist tyranny and let me feel the wickedness that gives that tyranny its strength. Though I did not understand it at the time, that day in my young life formed a kind of commission. My purpose on earth ultimately would become about the fight against socialist oppression in all its forms.

This, then, is my life. This is my battle. This is the story I am eager to tell.

I came into politics because I was devoted to a body of ideas. I know this defies the caricature. Conservatives are supposed to be from the country club set that comes to government to preserve its privileges, aren't they? They aren't supposed to have ideas. They are supposed to love profit and sing the praises of the free market. But ideas? No. Liberals expect conservatives to rape the land, oppress the poor, worship weapons, celebrate dictatorships, and make government the handmaiden of the rich.

Nothing could be further from the truth. In my case I had come to love a set of ideas, and these are what propelled me toward government.

These ideas were not new, though. They had been championed by Edmund Burke and John Adams, by Alexander Hamilton and Fisher Ames. They had been explained to my generation by William Buckley and C. S. Lewis, by Russell Kirk and Malcolm Muggeridge. And they had been thundered into the political marketplace of ideas during my lifetime by men like Barry Goldwater and Ronald Reagan.

These ideas are simple, and yet they so challenged the course of the twentieth century that they seemed radical when I first went to Washington.

There is a God and, because this is true, there is absolute moral truth.

Human life is not about the state but about God and his unfolding will for every individual.

Because men are flawed, governments should be kept small; should be bound by contracts with the people known as constitutions; and should be checked by an internal system of balanced powers.

Political power should be decentralized, so that state and local governments that are closest to the people have the greatest authority to shape their lives.

The free market works best to distribute goods and services. Government should stay out of the way.

Taxes are a necessary evil, and so should be kept small, fair, and few.

This way of life, this American system, should be protected by avoiding entangling international alliances; fiercely guarding the nation's borders; clinging tenaciously to the ways of the Founding Fathers; and making sure that all of these values are impressed on the next generation.

This is what I believed, and this is what I fought for. When I entered the United States House of Representatives in 1984 these ideas were the minority view. But things were changing, and by 1994 these views held enough sway in enough hearts to become the majority view. And thank God they did. Because of what has come to be known as the Conservative Revolution, life in America has been transformed. As I write these words early in 2007 I can attest that, because of the power of conservative ideas and the work of some political heroes willing to pay a price, the following is true:

- Every American now pays lower federal income taxes.
- Twenty-five million taxpayers receive a child tax credit.
- Thirty million married couples pay less in taxes, because of marriage penalty relief.
- Every serviceman and -woman in America is better equipped and better paid.
- The U.S. intelligence community has more spy satellites and more agents, and operates in more nations, than ever before in the nation's history.
- Some 2.3 million former welfare recipients have jobs; 3.5 million fewer families live in poverty; and 2.9 million fewer children live in poverty as a result of welfare reform.
- Some 17 million seniors over the age of sixty-five now have prescription drug insurance coverage they never had before.
- Every American can set aside tax-free money for unexpected health expenses.
- Partial-birth abortion—the practice of partially taking a child out of a woman's womb and then murdering it—is now illegal.
- The federal criminal appeals process has been streamlined, and the processes of prosecuting death penalty cases and carrying out a death sentence has been sped up.

The list of transforming policies based on conservative principles could go on for pages.* You see, the revolution was about the ideas, and the ideas won. They proved themselves. Whatever happens in the future, the enduring truth will be that conservative ideas changed American life for the better and proved that they could continue to do so if given the chance.

I am proud to have been a part of that revolution. I am proud of the changes we brought to government. We proved that the ways of the Founding Fathers work, and they work in a modern, high-tech world. In fact, we proved that the socialism that had been creeping into American society for decades was failing the American people, failing the American vision, and failing the challenges of a new millennium.

My own role in this revolution is a story I am eager to share, and not to say that I was the only soldier. If politics is the art of truth in pursuit of power, I am the man who builds the conduit from the truth to the power. I am not the charm. That is Newt Gingrich or Dick Armey. I am not the voice. That is Ronald Reagan, or perhaps Arnold Schwarzenegger, if the 2004 Republican convention is any indication. And I am also not the mind. No, I am the strategist who takes the ideas and builds a way for them to become law. As I'll explain in the coming pages, my gift is to see a need, and then to devise a system to answer that need. This is what I have done, and this is how I served the revolution. I took the ideas and worked them through the meat grinder of Congress, making a more efficient system of that meat grinder along the way. Because I was teamed with men of

---

*A more complete list of accomplishments can be found in Major Garrett's wonderful book *The Enduring Revolution: The Inside Story of the Republican Ascendance and Why It Will Continue* (New York: Three Rivers Press, 2005).

complementary gifts, we were phenomenally successful. What we accomplished was historic and ought to have continued for generations.

The reason it didn't continue, at least with my participation, is also a story that I am eager to tell. You see, I have learned something about liberals. They are much like communists. They believe they have to destroy you in order to win. This is because they are not about ideas. If politics is indeed the art of truth in pursuit of power, tyranny is the exercise of power apart from truth. This is liberalism as exemplified by Nancy Pelosi, Rahm Emanuel, Patrick Kennedy, and Jim McDermott, to name a few. These liberals in Congress have no ideas that history hasn't disproved, and this leaves them pursuing only power. To get that power, they will destroy you—*and if they can't destroy your message they will try to lock up the messenger.* Congress today is plagued by the politics of personal destruction, and this is why. To oppose a liberal is not to provide an alternative view. It is to commit a crime. It is to face prosecution by the self-anointed elite.

Today I find myself charged with money laundering by a local Texas district attorney, a partisan Democrat, who I'm convinced is doing the bidding of his political masters in Washington, D.C. The charge is false, of course, as I will prove in court if necessary, and explain in these pages, but I hope my story is a warning against the communist-style tactics of the left. We deserve better in America. If we are ever going to have people of integrity running for public office, we will have to bring the politics of personal destruction to an end. In the meantime, Congress has become a meaner and spiritually smaller place because liberalism is largely bankrupt of ideas, and has become primarily about grabbing power for its own sake. There is little grand vision, little noble ideal. There is the grasping for power and the will to destroy those who stand in the way.

This is how I came to the crisis that I have endured. I stood in the way of liberalism's grasp for power. In the present climate, this couldn't be tolerated. In the liberal mind, I had to be destroyed. Since the liberals did not have the character to defeat me with the power of ideas, they decided to defeat me in the courts. As I will explain in these pages, since 1996 there has been a coordinated effort to make me the poster boy for the culture of corruption in Washington. This effort has been led by Nancy Pelosi, Patrick Kennedy, Rahm Emanuel, and their henchmen, as well as by Martin Frost in Texas. Employing the media, incessant frivolous ethics charges, lawsuits, and disgraceful tactics on the floor of the House of Representatives, these conspirators have sought to drive me from office and destroy the Republican Revolution with the politics of personal destruction. I will explain later in this book the lies these conspirators have employed, and I will expose those lies with the truth. Such wickedness will ultimately fail, of course, but in the meantime we will see the tactics of a morally bankrupt liberalism playing themselves out. The sound you will hear while this farce unfolds is the death rattle of liberalism.

I, however, continue to be about ideas. They matter more than I do. They are the meaning of this nation and may well, if reclaimed, be the salvation of this nation. They are why I will not stop fighting, and why I plan to spend my days calling others to this same fight, even if I'm not doing it from Congress. In the story that fills these pages I trust the urgency of this fight will become clear.

I trust it will also become clear why I say these words: No Retreat, No Surrender. Not to liberalism. Not to the politics of personal destruction. Not to every type of Castro-like tyranny on earth. No Retreat. No Surrender.

MY POLITICAL MANIFESTO

I am not a man who apologizes for what he believes. This is because I did not create my beliefs, I received them: from the Bible; from great minds of the ages; from the experiences of nations; and from the principles of American freedom. Liberals may hate me for it, and weak-kneed Republicans may back away from it, but I cling to these ideas because I believe them to be true.

In the pages that follow I will tell you how I came to my beliefs, and how conservative ideas have worked time and again. First, though, I should tell you what these ideas are, for it is the ideas that give my political life meaning. Without these the story that unfolds in these pages is the tale of just another politician and just another movement fading into American political history. What must survive both me and our age are the ideas that have made America glorious in the past, and that will again if we reclaim them for our children's children.

Manifesto comes from the Latin word for "clear or evident." It means a public declaration of those things that are obvious or certain to a man or a movement. This is what Thomas Jefferson meant when he wrote "We hold these truths to be self-evident." This, then, is my manifesto, the body of ideas that I believe are clear and evident, and to which I have committed my life.

- There is a God, and he has made his will known. Because this is true, human life is not primarily about government or the state. It is about God and his unfolding plan for each individual.
- Because there is a God who has spoken, issues like marriage, abortion, homosexuality, and the death penalty are not matters of opinion. They are matters of revelation. There are moral absolutes and public policy should be built upon them.
- The Constitution of this country is a contract between the people and their leaders. Government should observe its constitutional boundaries and amendments should be made sparingly.
- Government should remain focused on the few things it does well. The dramatic expansion of the federal government in recent generations has come close to making slaves of the American people. Therefore, the federal government should be redesigned along constitutional lines:
    - Congress should be restored to primacy in the constitutional system.
    - The number of seats in the House of Representatives should be increased to reflect increases in population.
    - The executive branch should be reduced to the size and function intended by the Founding Fathers.
    - The judicial branch should be kept from activism through congressional restriction of judicial review; twelve-year term limits for judges instead of lifetime appointments; and impeachment of judges for unconstitutional actions and misconduct.
    - Congress should be allowed to overturn a U.S. Supreme Court ruling by a two-thirds vote.

- Senators should again be elected by state legislatures, as they were until 1913.
- The Departments of Education and Commerce should be eliminated, as should agencies such as the Environmental Protection Agency (EPA), the National Endowment for the Arts (NEA), the National Endowment for the Humanities (NEH), and the Occupational Safety and Health Administration (OSHA).
- The Department of Agriculture should be downsized, and the Department of Homeland Security should be completely overhauled.
- Spending for federal entitlement programs should not be renewed automatically but should be reviewed and reformed each year.
- All federal regulations interfering with the function of the free market in the United States should be repealed.

- The problem is not that too much money is spent on political campaigns in this country but that too little is. Americans spend more on potato chips than on putting competent leaders in office. All restrictions on campaign financing should be removed. There should be no limit on contributions, but instant reporting should be required.
- The First Amendment's Establishment Clause was designed to prevent a national church and federal preference for one religion over another. The misapplication of the Establishment Clause since *Everson v. Board of Education* should be reversed. The federal government should be allowed to support religion in general in order to fulfill its constitutional mission. Congress should restrict the judiciary from ruling in matters of religion, and leave those decisions to state and federal legislatures.
- The family is the building block of American society and should be protected by law and unmolested by taxes.

- Public schools should be reformed with urgency. School vouchers should be instituted; privatization should be introduced; and control should be returned to the state and local levels. The stranglehold of teachers' unions upon public education should be brought to an end.

- Abortion should be outlawed in America as the unjustified taking of a human life.

- Fundamental tax reform should commence immediately, with Congress creating a twenty-first century tax code of low, fair taxes. The Internal Revenue Service should be drastically reformed accordingly.

- Private property rights must be protected at all costs, particularly from takings through taxation, unjust eminent domain laws, illegal searches and seizures, or overregulation such as the Endangered Species Act.

- The United States should support unrestrained free trade worldwide.

- Given that the territorial integrity of a nation is essential to its survival, illegal immigration must be stopped through strong defense of America's borders and a restricted guest worker program.

- The United States should assure the safety and stability of the state of Israel.

- The American military should be retooled as far as necessary to reflect today's threats around the world. Opposition to terrorism should be a primary objective. The Strategic Defense Initiative (SDI) should be fully developed and deployed.

- No American should be sent to war without constitutional cause, clear objectives, and the best tools available to accomplish those objectives.

- No American serviceman or -woman should be placed under foreign or UN command.

• There should be a brief and factual annual report issued by the federal government each year justifying costs and objectives to the American people.

These principles are what I believe and what I have fought for during the three decades of my political life. I've learned in those three decades that having beliefs as strong as these—and the resolve to make them law—makes one a target.

RAISING MYSELF

I was born in 1947, a classic baby boomer with a blue-collar, South Texas twist. It was a momentous time to come into the world. That same year the term "cold war" was coined to describe the tense relationship between the United States and the Soviet Union. Not long after, President Harry Truman announced his intent to contain communism and General George Marshall announced his plan to strengthen Europe after the devastations of World War II. India and Pakistan both won their independence that year, and the United Nations voted to partition Palestine between Arabs and Jews. The Middle East—indeed, the world—was never the same again.

President Truman gave the first televised speech from the White House in 1947, and the proceedings of the U.S. Congress were also broadcast for the first time. It's been downhill ever since. On a nobler plane, Jackie Robinson transformed American sports when he crossed the color line to debut with the Brooklyn Dodgers baseball team and NASCAR, the true sport of kings, was born that year.

It was a banner year for liberals, too. On July 2, an object suspected of being a UFO was spotted over Roswell, New Mexico. Though the United States Air Force claims the object was a weather balloon, others insist this is a cover-up confirming the existence of a vast right-wing conspiracy. The founding myth of modern liberalism was thus born, held aloft not surprisingly by hot air and aliens.

When the stories of well-known men are told, there is usually an emphasis on the dramatic impacts of their parents. This is natural, I suppose, and fits a need to provide an explanation for the kind of man that the boy eventually became. Some have the experience of a Churchill, whose father hated him and who seems to have spent his whole life trying to outstrip this parental curse. Others are like Lincoln, who shared such a venomous relationship with his father that he refused to visit the man when he was dying. Then there are the more positive tales. John Wesley viewed his mother as his primary spiritual influence, and Theodore Roosevelt honored his father as his model of manhood.

Most stories fall into these two categories, either the *Mommy Dearest,* what-bad-things-my-parents-did-to-me type, or the *Father Knows Best* or *Leave It to Beaver* variety. But some of us had an experience of a completely different kind. Some of us had relationships with our parents that were so neutral or distant that we were virtually left alone. This is where I land, and when I say, as I often do, that I raised myself, I mean it without pride or anger. The fact is that my parents were so busy, distracted, or focused on their demons that I was left to learn the ways of the world on my own. I suspect there are many people in the world with similar stories.

My father, Charles Ray DeLay, grew up in Laredo, Texas, where his father, Ray, owned two machine shops that made tools and equipment for drilling oil. My mother grew up in Corpus Christi, about a hundred and fifty miles east of Laredo, where her father worked for the Humble Oil refinery there on the Gulf Coast. The two met at Texas College of

Arts and Industries in Kingsville, which they both attended in the early 1940s. Like many students of the time, though, they would never finish their studies. Life changed forever on December 7, 1941, when the nation of Japan bombed Pearl Harbor. In quick succession, Mom and Dad married and left Texas A&I, and Dad enlisted in the National Guard.

Dad dreamed of being a fighter pilot and was sent to train at Aloe Army Air Field in Victoria, Texas. He learned both to fly single-engine fighters and to shoot them down with ground and aerial gunnery. Dad was a good pilot. In fact, he was very good, but as graduation approached and he might have begun fulfilling his dream of fighting Nazis and the empire of Japan in the air, his superiors at Aloe learned that he was fluent in Spanish. This was an invaluable skill at the time. We often forget that Mexico was our ally in World War II, and that the United States agreed to train the Mexican Air Force to fly P-40 Warhawk and P-47 Thunderbolt fighters for deployment in the Pacific theater, where they were badly needed. The Mexicans distinguished themselves as pilots. Indeed, one squadron, the Aztec Eagles, earned a lasting reputation for valor during the Allies' air campaign over the Philippines. Because the Mexican pilots proved so valuable, and because there were few Spanish-speaking American instructors, my dad was assigned to train Mexican pilots rather than fly combat missions over Europe or the Pacific islands. Much to his disappointment, he spent the entire war in South Texas.

As Allied victories in Europe and the Far East began bringing peace to the world, my brother, Charles Ray, Jr. (called "Ray"), was born. In 1945, with the war's end, Aloe Field closed, and my dad left the service with his wife and child to return to his father's two machine shops in Laredo. Not long after, I was born. My earliest memory is of playing with the metal shavings on the floor of my grandfather's machine shop. I suppose that I might have spent the rest of my life working in those shops, or in something like them; I suppose the South Texas life of a machinist or an oil field worker might well have been mine. But God rules, and he often does so through the needs and ambitions of men. In my case, destiny intervened through my father's restless soul.

Dad was one of the most unusual men I have ever known. He was a natural engineer, was amazingly gifted with his hands, and had the ability to design and build almost anything. This combined with his independent, assertive, adventurous nature to make him an instinctive leader and entrepreneur. The price of these gifts was a painful inability ever to be satisfied, and there was no way he could settle for the life of an apprentice shopkeeper in Laredo, Texas. In 1953, when I was five, Dad decided he wanted to be a farmer, and he bought a spread in Mount George, Arkansas, a small town just outside of Dardanelles on the Petit Jean River. In a scene that would become familiar to all of us, Dad packed us into the family station wagon and headed north.

The DeLay farm raised maize and sorghum, but was mainly known for its chickens. Actually, it wasn't the chickens that brought us notoriety but the chicken house. Dad, the genius inventor, had rigged up an array of automated conveyor belts to feed and water the chickens every day at the appropriate times. It was an impressive, mystifying sight for the uninitiated. People came from miles around to see the DeLays' mechanized chicken house with its big rolling belts moving rhythmically under each contented chicken. Though it was nothing to compare with today's mechanized poultry operations, it was far more humane, and it was also a curious Disney-like innovation among the rather bland Arkansas farms of the day.

While Dad threw himself into the life of a farmer, I threw myself into boyhood. Like most children of my generation, I manufactured my entertainment with friends and imagination. We devised games of adventure, replayed scenes from the films of our day, and devoted ourselves to sports by the hour. I believe this awakened an inner creativity and drive that the passive entertainment of today—television and video games—only buries. I'm thankful I lived an outdoor, adventurous, energetic childhood that taxed my wits and challenged my body. I know it is natural for parents to believe that they lived their childhoods on a larger scale than their children do, but I really believe that people of my age knew something of an unplugged, all-American childhood that later generations will never know. Frankly, it saddens me.

One of my most enduring memories of these Arkansas years was learning how to smoke. There was a farmhand named Dakus who had two sons, Donnie and Kudu. No, I'm not making those names up. Donnie and I were friends, and one day we were walking down a dusty road having a smoke. We thought we were about as James Dean cool as we could be until I turned around and saw that the woman in the car passing by was my mother. She jumped out, scooped me up, and spent the drive home warning me of the agonies that would befall me at my father's hands.

My father's response to the news of my waywardness confused me at first. He didn't rage and he didn't punish. He calmly sat down with a carton of old-school, unfiltered cigarettes and told me he was going to teach me a lesson. My punishment would be to smoke all two hundred cigarettes in the carton. He was sure, he said, that this would teach me everything I would ever need to know about smoking.

Now I have heard similar stories so many times from friends of my age that I'm fairly sure some child-rearing expert must have been pushing this approach in the early 1950s. Maybe it worked with other children; it didn't with me. By the time I had smoked through two packs of cigarettes my father began lecturing me, a sure sign he sensed defeat. I had no intention of betraying the acrid, tarry fire burning in my mouth and chest. Finally, Dad stormed from the room and I knew I had won.

The farmers we knew would have used the word "contrary" of me at that moment. It was not the last time that people around me would notice that trait.

It was at this time in my life when I learned a few of the lessons that death has to teach. One of my playmates was a girl I remember as pretty and energetic. Without warning, a painful skin disease struck her, and she died quickly. I remember thinking about the indiscriminate, uncaring nature of what had happened. The girl had done nothing to deserve her fate. The same disease might have hit any of dozens of children in the area. Yet she was the one to fall. I remember noticing how the grown-ups took her death in stride, almost as though it were expected.

This was not my first experience with the death of a friend. Not too long before I had been playing with a friend in the street. We were chasing down cars and doing what boys often do: racing each other, seeing who could come closest to catching up to a speeding car. As we laughed and reveled in our antics, I heard a thud. I looked up to see my friend flying through the air like a rag doll. He landed a half a block away, and I still remember his mangled body, lifeless against the curb. He had been hit by a speeding truck in which the driver was seated too high to see a small boy running below.

I was not deeply introspective then, and I suppose I'm still not now. I do remember being aware of something entering my soul. It was a feeling that was like what I had seen on the faces of the grown-ups when my friend was struck down by disease. It was a sense of tragedy expected, of life as fragile and of pain as part of the plan. I have sometimes wondered if this isn't when maturity comes to a man, no matter his age. The moment he realizes that life is made up of light and dark, that grief and loss will come as surely as joy, he is mature in the only ways that truly matter. This happened to me early in life, and I'm glad it did, painful though the process was. We live differently when we know that life is not automatic, and I'm glad I did not come to that knowledge late in life.

By 1954 it had become obvious that the DeLay experiment in agriculture was failing. The defining moment came when my mother could not buy shoes for my younger brother, Randy. Not too long afterward, we crammed ourselves once again into the family station wagon—my father brooding about his failure, my mother brooding about our financial predicament—and we drove back to Texas. It was not a pleasant journey.

We did not return to Laredo, but instead landed in Corpus Christi, my mother's hometown. We were there only a year, and I remember two powerful experiences from that time. First, I fell in love. She was the prettiest thing I had ever seen, and her name was Catherine Grant. I was smitten. The moment I will never forget came one day at school behind a pink oleander bush during recess. The sun was out, the birds were chirping, and the blossoms were in full bloom. It felt right. I decided Catherine and I should take our relationship "to the next level." I made my move. I wrapped my arm around her lovely shoulder and pulled her close. She moved, though, and instead of what were surely sweet lips pressed to mine became instead an oleander branch to my eye. What should have been my first kiss became instead my first black eye. Oh, how the name of Catherine Grant has lived in infamy throughout my life.

The second tragedy to befall me that year was my older brother's doing. He informed me that there was no Santa Claus—a wound deeper than any Catherine Grant could have caused. My miseries seemed to be mounting, and when I was later told we would be leaving Corpus Christi, no news could have been more welcome.

My father had returned to the world of Texas oil just as the American lifestyle was creating a historic demand for petroleum. In the wake of World War II, the United States was prosperous and eager to emerge from sixteen years of economic depression and war. Returning service-men went to college on the GI bill, and then fanned out into the suburbs that were erupting around every city in America. These suburbs required cars, as did vacations to see America on the new Eisenhower-era super-highways that became all the rage in those years. Whether the average American thought about it or not, petroleum fed these trends, and it made products as diverse as rubber tires and bubble gum possible. It took no genius on the part of oil companies to see what the future meant to them, and they began scouring the earth for untapped reserves. This brought the vast resources of South America into focus, which in turn led to Charlie DeLay being hired by Atlantic Richfield to work in the oil fields of Venezuela. For the third time in my life and the second time in a year, my family packed all of its belongings into our old station wagon and set out for a new destination, in this case to New Orleans to catch a flight for Caracas.

From the moment we landed and settled into the Hotel Tamanaco in downtown Caracas, I felt as though I had stepped into a wonderland. For an eight-year-old boy to have the run of a fancy hotel in an exotic city is a gift to be treasured. I got to know maids, bellmen, doormen, the con-cierge, and the elevator operators who—if we begged—let us push the buttons on our own. We greeted the front-desk staff by name and were delighted to call down for room service or turndowns or "May we have more towels, please?" or "Can we get some extra blankets?" I'm sure we were a pain to the hotel management, but it was paradise for us.

A greater paradise awaited. Six months into our time in Venezuela, my father announced he had landed a better job with an oil firm called Helmerich & Payne as general manager of a drilling operation in the northern town of Tucupido. We soon learned that this meant we would be living smack dab in the middle of the Venezuelan rain forest, in a company town that is best described as small-town America trans-planted to the jungle. There Helmerich & Payne had built its own ver-sion of Andy Griffith's Mayberry, complete with single-family homes, stores, a community center, and even an open-air movie theater. To care for the oil men and their families, there were doctors and dentists, tradesmen and shopkeepers. Nothing, it seemed, had been overlooked.

It is hard to describe all these years later how life in this "camp" shaped me. Imagine my days as a nine-year-old boy in such a place. My conscious experience had been limited to an Arkansas farm and small, often dingy South Texas towns. Now I found myself, with budding curi-osity and physical courage, dropped into the middle of a South Ameri-can jungle! Because we were protected by a high, barbed-wire fence, the adults learned not to worry when we ventured out on our own. I was nearly as free then as a boy could be. What a world I had to explore! There were massive trees to climb and wild, exotic foliage to stir the imagination. And what wildlife! There were boa constrictors and igua-nas and huge, brilliantly colored birds. At the edge of the forest *caba-lleros* raised huge herds of cattle on South American–style ranches. Tom Sawyer and Huck Finn never had it so good. For me, Tucupido was heaven, or at least Eden before the fall.

Even the inconveniences of life in the camp conspired to produce good in my life. Our houses were actually Quonset huts, those all-purpose structures of rounded corrugated steel that the Navy had devel-oped during World War II. They were sweltering during the equatorial summers—not unlike living in the trunk of a car—and during the wet season they were like the inside of a steel drum. Rain in the Venezuelan jungle does not fall in torrents, it falls in bombardments. The drops are the size of walnuts, and they pummeled the uninsulated roofs of our huts for twelve hours at a time, often every day, and often for six months straight. The sound is deafening, and you learn to concentrate. I did, and the ability to focus completely and clear all distractions is one of the talents I cherish and rely on to this day.

This ability was also honed by the unique education I received during those years. Though I attended elementary school during the 1950s, I had the one-room schoolhouse experience that had been more common a century before. In a single classroom in Tucupido there were forty students who ranged from the first to the eighth grades. Each row of desks held a different grade. The teacher would stand in front of one row and teach a brief lesson, and then give the students in that row a short assignment. As they turned to their work, she then stepped to the next row and taught them. Strange as it sounds, this was the perfect system for me. Perhaps typically for boys my age, my attention span was short and constantly challenged. To have my lessons broken up into short bursts worked for me, and focusing through the constant activity in the room helped strengthen my powers of concentration.

My education spilled out of the classroom in those days and permeated my life in our jungle wonderland. My friends and I thought we were little Tarzans, lords of our rain forest kingdom, when in fact we were receiving an invaluable education. We learned about birds, snakes, lizards, and plants of every kind. We thought we were making a buck or two when we sold iguana eggs to the locals, but we were actually learning the ways of nature with a keenness most children never know. We built sprawling tree houses, learned local farming methods, and even absorbed the techniques of Venezuelan ranching from the *caballeros* nearby. When the locals held festivals, we joined in. On one occasion I led a traditional dance that the children put on for the adults. It was known as the Fish Dance, and for some reason that I can't recall, I was chosen to be the fish. My mother made a dramatic blue costume, complete with wildly flapping fins, and at the appropriate time children dressed as bears, monkeys, dogs, and lizards danced in a big circle with me, the fish, in the middle. Everyone cheered for "*Pesca* Tommy." I have often been thankful there were no pictures of the event for my political opponents to use against me.

The lessons I learned in those years have returned to me often throughout my life, some prompting a smile. I remember the day my dad came home from work with two saddles under his arms. I was beside myself with excitement. The saddles were child-sized and made of tanned leather, soft and shiny. Dad also led two burros, and it was then that my brother and I realized that our dreams of being real live *caballeros* were about to be fulfilled. Soon we were able to ride our own animals on our own saddles to the ranches nearby. We were just like the grown-ups—or so we thought.

One day I got separated from a group riding through the forest. It did not take long for the terror to strike me. Every sound signaled some horror to my eight-year-old ears, and I could envision my parents discovering my dead, partially chewed corpse days later. Each new direction looked right to me for a moment, and I led my burro this way and that until I was completely disoriented. My terror only increased. Then I had an idea. It occurred to me that my hungry burro might find his way home if I only let go of the reins and let him take over. So I did, and an hour later that sad-looking heap of bones shuffled into camp and took me right up to the door of our hut. There is a humorous lesson in the experience: In a crisis, don't ignore good ideas that come from a jackass.

I remember these years fondly not just for the beautiful setting and the thrilling childhood adventures, but because they were the best years of my family life. In my early years, anyway, my parents were loving and present, and our family life was not unlike the others that we knew.

Our idyllic lives in Tucupido were soon invaded by the horrors of Venezuelan politics. There had been political violence as long as we had been in the country, but we had ignored these tempests because they didn't seem to have much to do with our lives in the camp. In time, though, the ruling politicos realized that there was no place with greater protection from their enemies than the camps of the Western oil companies, and they began insisting on having homes within our safe haven. This made our camps targets, and I remember shuffling into the kitchen one day before school to find my father explaining to my brothers and sister that there had been a revolution, and that a lot of people had been killed. He said that Venezuela had a new government but that life for us would remain relatively normal.

Something about this didn't ring quite true later, when my family drove through town and saw bodies hanging from the streetlights in Tucupido's little town square. The local politicians had been murdered and then mounted for all to see. It got worse, though. The bodies hung there for weeks, reeking and swelling grotesquely in the equatorial heat. For fear of reprisals, no one cut them down. Finally, the bugs and birds having done their worst, the bodies just pulled apart and fell to the street below. Though I did not realize it at the time, this was the first in a series of ominous moments that would ultimately lead us out of Venezuela.

It was not long, though, before the ominous moments in my own family were of greater concern to me than anything going on in the camp. It was around this time that my grandfather Ray DeLay died in a car accident back home in Texas. My father was devastated and flew home to attend the funeral. My grandfather was a man loved and admired in Laredo. He was a leader both in his church and in his community, the kind of man people sought out for advice and learned to rely on for generosity and wisdom. So many people attended his funeral that they had to mount loudspeakers in the windows of the church so the crowds outside could hear.

When my father returned to Tucupido from the funeral, he was a changed man. I have learned that the death of a loved one sometimes changes the survivors in tragic ways, and in my father's case his grief led him to alcohol. Not long after returning, he was drunk every night. Though he did his job well during the day, he came home stumbling drunk long after our family had gone to bed. Sometimes he would come to my bedroom and try to tell me through slurred speech how he loved me, something he was incapable of expressing when he was sober. These experiences disgusted me, and I began to feel distant from a man I had once admired like no other. I realize now that a spirit had affixed itself to my family, and we began living out all of the dysfunctions so familiar to the families of alcoholics. Soon my brother began showing evidence of the same problem. Because the school in the camp only went to the eighth grade, my brother Ray was sent back to Texas to attend San Marcos Baptist Military Academy during his high school years. He fell in with the wrong crowd and began drinking. What began as teenage excess became a lifelong battle with alcohol.

Alcoholism destroys a man and a family from the inside out. This is particularly true when the alcoholic has the ability to appear normal at work or among friends. His family learns to enable the lie that all is well, and this makes the home a universe of dishonesty. Every relationship is tainted, distrust sets in, and people who once knew only love together find themselves drifting apart under the press of suspicion and fear. Each family member finds their own route of escape. My brother drank. My mother adopted an "Everything works out for the best" approach to life that only seemed like self-deception to me. And I gave in to my loner tendencies and pulled away into my own pursuits and pleasures. Though this served me well in many cases, I only narrowly escaped becoming an alcoholic myself. God alone knows the agonies that have been visited upon the human race through the abuse of alcohol.

While this cancer ate away at the core of our family, my father's career progressed beautifully. After two years in Tucupido, we were transferred about 450 miles southward to Santa Barbara, a midsized city that made our jungle lives look uncivilized. Our new camp was like a gated suburban community, with golf courses, swimming pools, and a schoolhouse so large that there were three grades per room rather than the eight I had known. I thrived here as I had in Tucupido, finding my first job selling popcorn at the camp's movie theater and gorging myself on the magnificent mangos that grew profusely in that area. I have still never eaten anything to rival the rich sweetness of that fruit.

Still, the political unrest of Venezuela haunted us. Having recovered from the cruelties of my first girlfriend, Catherine Grant, I now had another, who was the daughter of a local politician. The man kept a "safe house" inside our camp that was nothing compared to the sprawling estate he owned on the other side of town. There he housed many lizards and other fascinating specimens of the rain forest wildlife. His collection was a wonder, and I visited often.

That is what almost led to my death. One day my mother was startled by the sound of breaking glass, and she realized that a death squad was ransacking the politician's safe house next door in hopes of finding and killing its owner. Frantic, my mother looked for my brother and me throughout our house and all over camp to make sure we were safe. Without telling her, though, we had decided to visit the miniature zoo on the estate with my girlfriend. Unfortunately, having not found my girlfriend's father at his safe house, the death squad made its way to the man's estate—the same estate where I was with my brother and girlfriend. By the grace of God we left fifteen minutes before they arrived.

The next day we learned that the revolution that had begun the night before was particularly bloody. Everyone at my girlfriend's house, even the animals in the miniature zoo, had been slaughtered. I remember both my girlfriend's grief over the deaths in her family and my mother's relief that my brother and I were still alive. This was life as we knew it in the upheavals of Venezuelan politics.

Either because my parents requested it or my father's duties required it, we soon moved again, this time some four hundred miles northeast, to Anaco. It was easily the nicest place we lived in in Venezuela, and is notable in my memory as the site of my first foray into politics. It was a brash decision. I was a seventh grader, and I decided in my arrogant, loner style that I would challenge an eighth grader for president, though the job always went to a member of the higher grade.

I had an edge, though. My mother had taken to sending me home to Corpus Christi for several months every summer. Unfortunately, one of those months was May. So every year I finished school in Venezuela, and then had to go finish the last month of school in Texas as well. As it turned out, May was the month of student body elections, so each year I got to observe up close the way elections were done in the large schools in the States. By comparison, electioneering in our schools in Venezuela was stuck in the dark ages. These American schools had perfected the art of cardboard posters with rhyming slogans and candy giveaways. There were whole teams of campaigners and slick speeches. It was a wonder to behold, real state-of-the-art stuff! I carried these advanced techniques back to the comparatively sleepy political arena of Anaco and took the school by storm. My opponent didn't know what hit him! See: intelligence, technology, clear values, and voter turnout—I've been preaching these lessons ever since!

My life in Anaco was happy externally. We lived in luxury, my father having moved up the ladder of pay and responsibility. I caddied at the camp country club and, in afternoons when the older men found it too hot to play, I played for free, and became a pretty fair golfer. I had good friends, plenty to do, and, of course, there was always the raucous world of school politics to fill my time.

All of this hid the tragic truth that alcoholism was terrorizing our family. Dad's drinking grew even worse, making him abusive and vile. When my hard-drinking brother came home on vacations from military school, the two fought violently. Mom made do. I pulled away, becoming increasingly self-reliant and distant. I'm told the children of alcoholics learn to make the best of any situation, so much so that they come to deny that their horrible circumstances even exist. I may well be subject to this dysfunction. As I look back I remember the good of our years in Venezuela—and they were indeed glorious—but I have difficulty re-membering the dark seasons of anger and pain. This is either the grace of God or the symptom of a disease, but either way my memories are largely happy, and I am grateful this is so. It all came to an end in 1959, though, because there was another revolution. This one again cut too close to home, and with the strain of my father's drinking and the fear of the political horrors around us, my mother drew the line. We were going back to Texas.

What happened next has lived brightly in family lore. My father was unable to find a job when we returned to Corpus Christi. He had gained too much experience in Venezuela for the low-level oil jobs that were available back home. Mom and Dad had saved plenty of money due to the low cost of living in the company camps, but this couldn't last forever, and Dad needed to find a job. It was just then that Dad met Ralph and Jimmy Storm, owners of Storm Drilling Company. Storm was a modest company of small barges, small rigs, and small contracts that in the fall of 1959 was in bad shape. They weren't able to make payroll, and my father found out about it. In an astonishingly bold move, Dad walked into the Storm brothers' office and offered ten thousand dollars of his savings for a job as a drilling supervisor. It was an offer they couldn't refuse. This was Dad's opportunity for fortune, and he seized it. Within ten years he helped Storm Drilling open operations all over the Gulf of Mexico, Newfoundland, Peru, and the Canary Islands. He eventually orchestrated a buyout of the Storm brothers, was named president of the company, and by the 1980s had become a wealthy man.

In 1959, all of this was part of an unknown future. I was twelve and more focused on settling into a new school than on my father's career. My claim to fame in those days was my involvement in a junior high gang called—get ready for this one—"The Broken Pistons." We tried to be Fonzi-style cool, but the fact is that all the members of this gang were dorks just like me. For all my posing I made straight As, had a mouth full of braces, and played the coronet and the flügelhorn in the school band. There was absolutely nothing cool about me.

In fact, the most important thing about me in those years was political. Congressman Henry Hyde likes to say that it was a woman who turned him into a Republican—Eleanor Roosevelt; for me it was Miss Tennyson, my eighth-grade social studies teacher. In the weeks leading up to the 1960 presidential election she gave us an assignment to read the platforms of the two major political parties and write an essay about why we preferred one or the other. It may sound odd, given that I was so young, but when I read the Republican platform I saw the first expressions of what would become many of my dearest political thoughts: the unrelenting anticommunism; the commitment to a strong national defense; the call for personal responsibility and away from a welfare state; and, most of all, the confidence in a free market over command economics. I soon added a Nixon button to my very uncool and now Republican Broken Pistons jacket.

My newfound political views played into my love for reading. I tore through every book in the Hardy Boys series, of course, but my favorite book back then was John Steinbeck's *Grapes of Wrath*. I suppose I related to the characters because my own family had seen tough times, and because the images of a family on the move to find work reminded me of our experience. I was haunted, though, by the way the family in the book, the Joads, was treated. Here they were not looking for a handout but just trying to survive, and yet they were treated like dirt. Something in that book about man's capacity for injustice and cruelty hit me, and has never really left. The book and the 1940 John Ford/Henry Fonda movie it inspired both remain among my favorites.

In 1962, I moved for the sixth time in my life. This was because my parents had become concerned that my older brother and I had already begun drinking and carousing in Corpus Christi. We had definitely fallen in with the wrong crowd, and our characters were on the line. Hoping to find a healthier environment for us, my parents moved us fifteen miles west, to the town of Calallen.

Though it may sound odd, I can tell you exactly what I looked like my first day at Calallen High School. I apparently strutted like a peacock. I was wearing an old-school, Tex Ritter–style western shirt that was black with blue roses all over it. My sleeves were rolled up high to show what I thought were my bulging biceps. I wore incredibly tight jeans and sported sharp-toed, shiny shoes with white socks—just the fashion.

How do I know all this? Well, it turns out there was a girl watching me closely, and she told me all the details. Her name was Christine Furrh. Now Christine was easily the prettiest girl in the school. She was also one of the best students and one of the most gifted athletes, and she was known for her skills in the rodeo. I was struck by how down-to-earth she was, how she seemed to value everyone and not worry about being cool. We became good friends, and I even got along with her boyfriend, Ronnie "Frog" McCullough. In fact, when Ronnie found out he was moving to Arizona, he asked me to look after Christine for him. I was all too happy to fulfill his request, and was just making plans, when Christine walked up to me one day and asked me to the Sadie Hawkins dance. I said yes, and from the night of that dance I knew Christine was the love of my life. It is hard to explain, but Christine seemed to deal with me not as I was but as she knew I could be. This made me want to be the man she envisioned. When I say this, I don't mean anything sexual. I mean she helped me grow up. In fact, she is still helping me all these decades later.

If Christine was the beginning of my manhood, the 1964 presidential election was the beginning of my political maturity. I can still remember my conservative epiphany as though it happened yesterday. It was July 13, 1964, and I was sitting in our living room in Calallen, Texas, watching the flickering black-and-white images of the Republican National Convention broadcast from the Cow Palace in San Francisco. My interest in politics was nothing new, thanks to the influence of caring teachers, but I was unprepared for what was about to happen to me. After the usual speeches and convention business, a man named Senator Barry Goldwater strode to the rostrum. It is hard for me to describe what happened as he spoke. Perhaps his words should come before my attempt to explain.

The good Lord raised this mighty Republic to be a home for the brave and to flourish as the land of the free—not to stagnate in the swampland of collectivism, not to cringe before the bully of communism. . . .

And this party, with its every action, every word, every breath, and every heartbeat, has but a single resolve, and that is freedom. . . .

This nation and its people are freedom's models in a searching world. We can be freedom's missionaries in a doubting world. But, ladies and gentlemen, first we must renew freedom's mission in our own hearts and in our own homes. . . .

Those who seek to live your lives for you, to take your liberty in return for relieving you of yours, those who elevate the state and downgrade the citizen, must see ultimately a world in which earthly power can be substituted for divine will. And this nation was founded upon the rejection of that notion and upon the acceptance of God as the author of freedom. . . .

And I needn't remind you—but I will—it has been during Democratic years that a billion persons were cast into Communist captivity and their fate cynically sealed. . . . Today, today in our beloved country, we have an administration which seems eager to deal with communism in every coin known—from gold to wheat, from consulates to confidence, and even human freedom itself. . . .

I believe that the communism which boasts it will bury us will instead give way to the forces of freedom.

My fellow Republicans, we do no man a service by hiding freedom's light under a bushel of mistaken humility. I seek an America proud of its past, proud of its ways, proud of its dreams, and determined actively to proclaim them. But our examples to the world must, like charity, begin at home. Anyone who joins us in all sincerity, we welcome. Those, those who do not care for our cause, we don't expect to enter our ranks, in any case. And let our Republicanism so focused and so dedicated not be made fuzzy and futile by unthinking and stupid labels. I would remind you that extremism in the defense of liberty is no vice! And let me remind you also that moderation in the pursuit of justice is no virtue!

In a matter of less than an hour, my world changed forever. This man seemed to know my mind, to speak my language. He was no Nixon or Rockefeller. He was certainly no Kennedy or Johnson. He was a man with guts, speaking truth in plain language designed not to impress people but to lead them. He clearly wanted to break from the pack of "more of the same" Republicans. He offered an alternate world. America is good, communism is bad. Freedom is good, big government is bad. Strength is good, weakness is bad. Clarity is good, ambiguity is bad. The phrases resonated in my soul: "swampland of collectivism"; "bully of communism"; "extremism in defense of liberty."

Sitting on our couch, fixated on that flickering black-and-white image, I knew I belonged to something. This man's square jaw and angular, black glasses only added to an image of command and nonconformity that called to me. And there, at that convention, were people who thought as he did—as I did. I understood. I'm a conservative. This man had sounded a clear trumpet, and everything in me rose to the call. It still does.

Over the years people have often asked me why I had to become a Republican. After all, in the 1960s Texas was full of conservative Democrats who were as anticommunist and as in favor of free enterprise as Goldwater. Why couldn't I just feel at home with them? The reason is that conservative Democrats want to do conservative things through big government. I want to shrink the size of government. I think that government is part of the problem. This was Goldwater's position, and why he so captivated me. He said he wasn't interested in streamlining government or making it more efficient. He wanted to reduce its size. This was my brand of conservatism, and it defines me to this day. In fact, it is what distinguishes me from George W. Bush and his "compassionate conservatism." He wants to achieve conservative goals with liberal doses of government. I want to reduce the size of government and free the people to achieve their own goals. This was the dream I began to carry in my heart when I heard Goldwater speak in 1964.

This conservative epiphany occurred in the summer before my senior year of high school. It has shaped me ever since. I place it next to those hours at the Havana airport in 1959 as among the defining moments of my life. While my family seemed stuck in perpetual orbit around my father's drinking, and the swirl of 1960s America was gathering speed, I had found a worldview that gave me both meaning and belonging. This, along with my deepening relationship with Christine, propelled me forward as a man and as an American. In time my values and my relationship with Christine would bring me into conflict with both my father and the prevailing tide of my country. In 1964, though, my beliefs were both a comfort and a mission, much as they are today.

DESTINY RULES

In every life of consequence there are turning points. Call them "moments of destiny," call them "the road less traveled," or call them "defining decisions," they are the turning points that determine everything that comes after. One of mine came following a medical school interview in 1970.

Understanding this requires some background. My father had always insisted that one of his sons should be a doctor, one a lawyer, and one a veterinarian. It was more than a wish. He worked at this dream. He burned it into our minds. When he was drunk he even tried to bribe us into taking the paths he had chosen for us.

You would think that my disgust for my father's drunken ways would cause me to reject his plan for my life. This is a natural expectation, but it ignores one of the horrible truths of alcoholism. Even though the child of an alcoholic knows that his parent is sick, he still tries to please. The greater the distance of the alcoholic parent, the harder the child works to win approval. This is what I did. Though my father's drunkenness disgusted me and ruined our family, I nevertheless tried to please him by preparing to go to medical school.

The foolishness of it all didn't really strike me until I went to an entrance interview for Tulane University Medical School. Now I suspect that my father had pulled some strings to make this interview happen. My grade point average was only 2.8, and no self-respecting medical school would have taken my application seriously. I think the man conducting the interview knew I wasn't qualified and knew that the meeting was a political favor. This may explain why he was so vicious.

The meeting turned sour after only a few minutes, when the man asked me what I was reading. I answered that I was just finishing *Gone With the Wind*. "Mr. Tulane" was incredulous. He began screaming at me that if I was going to get into medical school I was going to have to read more serious literature than that. He told me that I was worthless, and that the idea of medical school for me was laughable.

The interview continued in this tone for a while longer before I left. I was hurt, frustrated, and angry. Yet it wasn't just the interview. It was that the interview seemed as bad as the whole idea of going to medical school in the first place. It just wasn't right. It was the programming of a man who did not know me and did not respect my gifts, and who wanted my life to be a trophy to his vanity. I went and told Christine the truth I should have acknowledged long before: I did not want to be a doctor. She was amazing. Though our lives were about to pivot on a dime, she said, "Well, you don't have to be a doctor. There are other options." With those words she opened the door to possibilities I had not considered.

Within days I had informed my father of my decision, closed the door to medical school, and begun looking for another career. The most important change, though, had been in my own soul. I had chosen, and against the insistence of my father, chosen what I knew to be right. This was as important as the decision itself, but both the freedom to choose and the path chosen has made the difference every day since. I was learning the ways of destiny.

* * *

I should have known something was wrong that morning in 1965 when I woke up for my first day at Baylor University. I had enrolled in Baylor because they had a good biology program, and biology, I knew, would lead to medical school. Baylor's reputation as a hotbed of religious fundamentalism didn't trouble me at all. I had been sidestepping religion for years.

In fact, I had even been baptized, and it hadn't really done me any harm. When my family returned from Venezuela, we attended Parkdale Baptist Church in Corpus Christi, and I remember that I was sitting in the back of the service with my friends one day when I noticed my family walking down the center aisle toward the front. I jumped up and followed them forward, and a few minutes later realized that we were all supposed to affirm our faith in Jesus Christ. I said the words, got baptized, and was welcomed by all as a Christian. The truth is I was baptized a thorough pagan. Though I probably benefited from the excellent Bible teaching at Parkdale over the next years, I never really possessed a true faith of my own in those days.

That's what made my first morning at Baylor such a shock. I awoke to something horrible ringing in my ears. Through my sleepy haze I realized it was music. No, not music: hymns. There were hymns playing on the record player in my dorm room! Then it got worse. My two roommates were singing those hymns aloud, sometimes adding prayers and hallelujahs. The room was spinning—religiously. Then it hit me. Though I had come to Baylor hoping to escape its more religious edge, this was not to be my fate: I was rooming with Peter and Paul.

Something had to be done; these Baptists were not to be trifled with. If you didn't take a stand, you might get sucked in. I decided to declare myself. I went out and joined the Esquires, a fringe social club that would have been a fraternity except that fraternities weren't allowed at Baylor. These Baptists were too strict to permit such things. There was even a joke about it: Baptists didn't believe in premarital sex because it might lead to dancing.

In such an environment I was bound to get tangled up in the rules eventually, and it happened the first of many times during the third week of October that first year. Everyone at Baylor was gearing up for the big homecoming game against Texas A&M. It was called "rivalry week," and the whole school was on guard against the strategic vandalism that often graced the occasion. In fact, Baylor's entire freshman class—easily identified by the green-and-gold beanies they were traditionally required to wear—was responsible for campus security. "Slime," as we were graciously called by the upper classmen, were posted twenty-four hours a day against Aggie infiltration.

On the Thursday night of that week I was on duty with some of my friends when word came of a desecration. We hurried to the other side of the campus to see the horror: Some evil being had spray-painted a maroon-and-white A&M logo on Baylor's administration building. My friends were furious. I was inspired. I rounded up eleven Esquires and all the beer we could get our hands on and headed down Highway 6 the eighty miles to College Station. Somehow, cans of green-and-gold spray paint accompanied us. The details aren't important. It is enough to say that by dawn Friday a green-and-gold "BU '69" adorned every single building on the Texas A&M campus.

Our plan had been executed flawlessly, and we escaped without notice. As we drove home celebrating our accomplishment, we noticed a single car with a Baylor sticker heading back toward A&M. We tried to signal them but they sped by, and we thought nothing further of it. The next morning we learned what had happened. A friend's roommate— a Bible-thumping, goody two-shoes, hymns-in-the-morning type—had learned what we had planned for the Texas A & M campus and had driven to College Station to stop us. Unfortunately, he had arrived just as the Aggies were waking up to the decoration of their campus. He was arrested and squealed like a pig about the heathen friend and his eleven disciples of evil.

I was put on probation and marked by the administration as a certain source of trouble. In the spring of 1967 I lived up to those expectations. I had been handed the task of planning the Esquires' formal, the crowning event of Baylor's unofficial social calendar. The responsibility was a high honor, and I laid all the plans carefully. I rented the nicest ballroom at the nicest hotel in Waco. I hired the band, ordered the food, and even made sure that the "booze room" was chosen wisely and properly stocked. Raids by the administration were always anticipated, and the booze room was rented privately so that Baylor students could enjoy a non-Baptist drink without violating the rules.

My downfall that night was my choice of date. Now Christine and I were still dating, but she was 170 miles east of Waco, attending Panola Junior College. I knew she was my love and my soul's anchor, but no true chairman of the Esquires' formal could go without a date. So I asked, er—well, let's call her Jane, for reasons that will be obvious as the story unfolds. Jane had just broken up with, er—let's call him Dick, again for reasons that will be obvious—and I thought she might need some encouragement. After all, she had faked a suicide attempt when the breakup occurred. I felt certain that being the date of the party chairman could only be the thrill of a lifetime and would cheer her up.

The evening unfolded beautifully. The band, the food, and the guests were all stunning. My well-chosen booze room had escaped administration snoops successfully, and all was proceeding perfectly. Then it happened, and it wasn't even my fault. Jane's Baptist preacher father apparently had been told that his daughter was depressed over her breakup with Dick, and so he had rushed to Waco to comfort her. He arrived at the party desperate to find his bereaved daughter. Jane, however, had encountered Dick on the dance floor, and the two had reignited. I must have been somewhere tending to party details. By the time Dad found Jane, though, she was in the booze room. With Dick. In bed. Reconciling.

None of this was necessarily bad news for me. I didn't have any serious designs on Jane, and the existence of the booze room was a well-known secret on campus that frankly couldn't be traced to any one student anyway. Dick and Jane were clearly in trouble, but that idea wasn't going to keep me up at night either. She was my date, after all, and Dick should have maintained the honor of the Esquires and kept his reconciling for another time. My trouble came when Jane's fuming father demanded to know the name of the boy she was in bed with. She took a deep breath, looked up at him sweetly, and said, "Tom DeLay."

From that moment my days at Baylor were numbered. By the end of spring semester 1967, I had been informed that my presence on campus was no longer required. It didn't matter as much as it might have, though, because I had already decided that Christine and I should be married. She was absolutely the love of my life, and there was no sense putting up with the Janes of the world any longer. Christine and I were engaged that summer and set the wedding for August 26, and I worked as a roustabout on one of my father's oil rigs. Meanwhile, I searched for a school that would admit me just weeks before my junior year. Thankfully, the University of Houston was willing. So, after our sweet wedding, Christine and I began a life of student newlyweds: She worked at an insurance office and I attended classes, laboring in the athletic department's laundry service after hours. Our refrain was the stuff of country music: We were poor but in love.

It took me three years to finish at the University of Houston because some of my Baylor credits did not transfer. This is why I graduated in

1970, and why that decisive interview with that discouraging man from Tulane did not occur until that same year.

As free as I felt from my father's insistence that I become a doctor, I then faced the question of what I would do with my life. It was discouraging to learn that there were few jobs for biology majors. Christine suggested that I contact a headhunter and tell him my predicament. Once again, her advice changed my life. The step I took based on that meeting ultimately led me into politics.

The headhunter told me of a company called Redwood Chemical that was looking for a manager. It was a family-owned business that sold chemicals and supplies to pest-control businesses in Texas and the surrounding states. It also sold chemicals retail at discount prices from a storefront in downtown Houston. Tragically, the company's founder, K. P. Glasse, recently had been murdered during a store robbery. K.P.'s son, Buddy, took over the day-to-day operations but needed someone to fill his former role. This became my first job after college.

My first six months at Redwood Chemical were the worst of my life. Buddy Glasse wanted his new manager to learn the business from the bottom up, and I didn't resist. I loaded and unloaded boxcars. I worked in the warehouse among the worst fumes and toxic chemicals imaginable. I poured chemicals, made pesticides, worked the storefront, and cleaned every surface again and again. In the evenings I went home reeking, but those torturous months taught me valuable lessons. First, I learned the pesticide business from the inside out. I learned how to mix chemicals, how to treat a home, which chemicals kill which kinds of insects, and what kind of environment usually hosts what kind of pest. Perhaps as important, though, I learned that knowledge is power, and that if you master the details you gain a measure of control.

Redwood Chemical was a member of the Texas Pest Control Association (TPCA), which provided continuing education and training programs.

I went to so many of these sessions that before long I was teaching them. I also took correspondence courses in every aspect of the business. I studied biology, entomology, chemistry, and everything about the money and marketing side of pest control. It was not so much that I was fascinated with the exterminating business but that if I was going to do something, I wanted to do it well and know it thoroughly. I am one of those strange people who actually enjoys reading instruction manuals. I like knowing how things work, and understanding what is supposed to happen before I get down to business. I'm not just talking about bugs here. I'm talking about how there is power in knowing, and how I have often acquired power simply by taking the time to learn a process thoroughly.

This is a key to understanding who I am. Benjamin Disraeli once said, "The secret of success is constancy of purpose." My gift is this very constancy. Once I determine my goals, I orchestrate the hours of my day to achieve them. I spend my time getting better at whatever skill I need to achieve them. This requires the fine art of self-education. I take a long look at the mechanisms in place—in politics, pest control, or life in general—and then I read and ask questions until I know the details of the process. Once I master the process I feel comfortable not only working it but changing it if need be. This is my brand of leadership, a brand not based on looks or charm or brilliance, but on hard work, mastery of the details, and constancy of purpose.

My passion to improve might well have brought me into painful conflict with the Glasse family. I was ambitious and yearned to see Redwood Chemical achieve greatness with me in tow. The company was taking in nearly $6 million a year then, enough to give the Glasse family a comfortable lifestyle—and just enough to leave me wanting more. Buddy Glasse was a gifted innovator who often developed new pieces of equipment that I thought were easily marketable. I urged him to have the inventions manufactured and marketed professionally. But he was content to produce the parts himself. Clearly we had different dreams, and these might have led to a breach had we not had plenty to agree upon in the matter of politics—pest-control politics, that is.

In 1972 the Texas legislature began considering legislation that would have meant unprecedented regulation of the pest-control industry. This legislation was part of a trend of environmental activism, encouraged in large part by the birth of the Environmental Protection Agency (EPA), a gift to America from the Nixon administration two years earlier. Under pressure from environmentalists, the Texas pest-control industry was being threatened with government-sanctioned licensing requirements for pest-control operators. Previously the pest-control industry in Texas had a free market. Competition had kept prices down, service levels high, and safety the top priority. Yet without any evidence that the pest-control industry had failed to police itself adequately, liberals were urging extremely restrictive licensing requirements. This would have meant little increase in safety, higher prices, and the birth of an expensive bureaucracy to monitor the industry.

All of this was being attempted in the name of environmental protection. The reality, however, is that in the same way that nature abhors a vacuum, liberalism abhors a free market. The real issue wasn't protecting Texas from mishandled pesticides; the real issue was protecting Texans from freedom. Environmental activism is just socialism in disguise. Columnist George Will calls it "collectivism in drag." The true aspiration of the environmentalist fringe is not a *clean* ecosystem, but a *cleansed* political system, purified of toxins like individualism, self-reliance, and competitive economics.

Buddy Glasse worked hard in Austin to defeat this unnecessary legislation. He took time from growing his own business to coordinate lobbying efforts, organize the TPCA's members, and talk sense to the state's legislators. He and others like him were ultimately defeated, and the pest-control industry in Texas became bloated and corrupt. Years later, when I was in the state legislature, I found that the pest-control businessmen had become addicted to regulation and were proposing legislation to heighten licensing regulations in order to prevent new businesses from entering their market. In other words, they had realized that regulation restricts competition, and they had decided to use these restrictions for their own benefit. The environmentalists had taught them well. Fortunately, I was in a position to defeat this scandalous effort, and I did.

The battle against the regulation of pest control in Texas was a vital political education for me. I was already a philosophical conservative, but watching liberalism's cynical grasp for power alerted me to the urgency of my ideas. What I saw was what Barry Goldwater had thundered against that night in San Francisco in 1964, what Ronald Reagan had talked about every week in his radio commentaries, what William Buckley, Jr., and his writers were decrying in the pages of *National Review.* The philosophical integrity of conservatism had run headlong into the tactical power of liberalism and, in that instance as in thousands of others in that era, we were routed. All around the country in the late 1960s and early 1970s, this story was being repeated.

Having some sense of the critical issues in play at the time, I launched into an aggressive program of political self-education. I read books on national and state politics, and I devoured *National Review* and *Human Events* from cover to cover. I never missed Reagan's radio commentaries, and I listened carefully as Christine fed me from the books she read. She has a much greater mind than I have, and she is also a gifted teacher. She would read works from Machiavelli to Goldwater, and from Plato to Buckley, patiently explaining the seminal ideas from each one to her slower husband. My devotion to conservativism became both more practical and more profoundly philosophical during those years, thanks to mean-spirited liberalism and kindhearted Christine.

While I grew philosophically, I also yearned to grow economically. Our daughter, Danielle Kay, was born in 1972, and this event had begun to change how I looked at my life. Having a child awakens something in a man. He starts thinking about his life in terms of the next generation and how he will provide for it. Once I held Dani in my arms, I could no longer be satisfied with just paying the bills and putting food on the table. I wanted to earn enough to pay for the life I could envision when I looked into that little face. Most men feel this same surge of determination when they hold their first child in their arms, and thank God they do: It is one of the great engines of human progress.

I was already feeling these fatherly yearnings when I ran into a friend from high school and we pulled aside to talk. He told me he was managing a convenience store in downtown Houston and was making $1,000 a month, $150 more than I was making managing a $6 million business. The scales fell from my eyes. I went to Buddy and told him I wanted at least $1,000 per month, a company car, and 5 percent of Redwood's profits. He countered with $950 a month, a secondhand car that the Glasse family kept in a barn, and no profit sharing. No deal. I gave my two weeks' notice.

Christine and I had already decided that if I did not continue with Redwood I would go into business on my own. After three years in the industry, I felt I could do well. I made a big mistake, though. Inspired by what some at the time called "green chic," I chose to name my new venture Environmental Services. I did not do market research, and so I did not know that people would think I was just another government agency. Besides, people gravitate to names they know and can trust, like McDonald's or the Gap. That's why the most successful new ventures are franchises of larger companies. My badly named little independent was suspect from the beginning, and it became a colossal flop.

Fortunately, a man I had known from my years at Redwood was getting older and was looking for someone to buy out his interest in a company called Albo Pest Control. I immediately saw my opportunity, secured a business loan, and bought the business. It was a wise move. Within months I went from failing to being moderately successful—largely because of the name change. Albo also had four trucks, six employees, and a good list of regular clients. We began to prosper. I bought a house thirty miles west of Houston in Valley Lodge, complete with a barn, attached stables, and a backyard so huge that I fenced it in for Christine's new horses.

Given my drive, gift for self-education, and management skills, I think I could have grown Albo into a significant company. The truth is that politics kept calling. Even my business life became a political education. Like all business people, I was aghast at how much government regulations interfere with the free market. I decided at one point to compute how much government was costing my business. I came to the conclusion that government was costing me 60 percent of my income. It occurred to me that most business people spend time trying to lower their costs but spend no time trying to lower the cost of government to their business. This truth wouldn't leave me alone. It constantly intruded itself into my consciousness, even though I didn't quite know what it meant for me.

What also kept gnawing at my mind was the pitiful state of the Republican Party in Texas at the time. Its desiccation was a symptom of a broader national disease. The fact is that the Republican Party in the United States offered no viable political alternative to Democratic one-party control. True, there were signs of a shift in American politics away from the utopian liberalism of Lyndon Johnson's Great Society, but as a rule Republican leaders still based their appeal to the American people on the idea that they would do exactly what the Democrats did, only they would do it better. The Republican Party was not yet a party of ideas. The party's electoral coalition, which regularly won about 30 to 40 percent of all congressional seats, was not animated by any core principles. The dynamic Republican Party of Ronald Reagan—defined by peace through strength; prosperity through smaller government and lower taxes; support for the unborn; and unrepentant American exceptionalism— was yet to announce itself.

Making this condition worse was what passed for Republican victories in the postwar era. The fact is that Eisenhower and Nixon were the furthest thing from conservatives in the Goldwater-Reagan-Thatcher mold. Their Republicanism wasn't about ideas, it was about personnel. They seemed to be saying to the nation that Republicans ought to be in office because they could run the Democrats' programs better than the Democrats could. No one seemed to be talking about fundamental change, though. This is why by the late 1970s what passed for a two-party system in Texas was actually on the one hand an entrenched, ideologically motivated Democratic Party that held almost every office in the state and, on the other hand, a Republican Party that offered no alternative ideas or strategies. Compounding this was the built-up resentment against Republicans that still existed in former Confederate states. In short, no one took Texas Republicans seriously in the mid-1970s because the Republicans didn't take themselves seriously.

There is no better confirmation of this fact than the story of how I became a precinct chairman. In 1976 I drove to Justice of the Peace Paul Till's office to take my brother to lunch. He was clerking for the judge at the time, and as I waited in the lobby I gave into a bad habit of mine—lecturing the television. This particular day I was telling the television how bad liberal politicians were after one of that breed had just sounded off on the tube. The receptionist overheard me and suggested that I stop complaining and do something about it. I did not know that she was the vice chairman of the Harris County Republican Party. A few days later I got a phone call from the local chairman telling me that I had been named the precinct chairman for Valley Lodge. In other words, as soon as I was identified as a living, breathing Republican—a rarity in that part of Texas—I was automatically considered a senior member of the local party leadership.

I had no idea what I was supposed to do. Thankfully, the job came with an instruction manual. It was entitled, appropriately enough, "How to Be a Precinct Captain." The whole situation was tailor-made for me. There was a goal, a role, and an instruction manual. Life couldn't get any better. Never mind that there were only five Republicans in our precinct. The handbook said to canvass the community, so I canvassed the community. It said to drop literature, so I dropped literature. It said to knock on doors, register voters, catalog respondents, and get contact information and keep it in an index card file. Step by step I grew the list of names— from five to more than one hundred, a 2,000 percent increase! The next chapter in the book detailed the means by which a precinct captain identifies and arranges the meeting place for the primary election. Unfortunately, the authors of the book had never been to Fort Bend County, where no Republican had been elected since Reconstruction . . . *to anything.*

I approached my pastor and asked if we could hold the primary in his church. He said no, explaining that if he let Republicans vote there, nobody—meaning Democrats—would ever come to his church. Then I stopped at a local strip mall that had three empty storefronts. I approached the owner of the property and asked if I could clean up one of the storefronts and host the primary there. No, I was told, if people knew Republicans had voted there, nobody would rent the stores again. I got the same answer at the Valley Lodge Club and a dozen other places. It was as though we were lepers and no one wanted to catch our disease. Finally, I decided to borrow a few card tables and hold the primary in my barn. On Election Day more than 160 people voted in my makeshift primary, and Ronald Reagan won, sweeping the Simonton, Texas, presidential primary of 1976. Republicanism was back from the dead.

It was during the next year, in 1977, that another decisive turning point occurred in my life. It did not begin gloriously. I was in the middle of a four-day continuing education seminar at Texas A&M. I arrived home exhausted one evening to hear Christine announce that the county chairman had called to tell me of my appointment to the Fort Bend County Republican Candidate Committee. There was a meeting that night. Great. Another meeting. I told Christine I wasn't going, but she insisted I fulfill my responsibilities. Angry, I put on some casual clothes inappropriate to the occasion and I stormed out. I drove the forty-five minutes to Sugar Land and spent several hours begging candidates to place their names on the ballot. As the evening drew to an end, the wife of the county chairman turned to me and joked, "Why don't you run for state representative?"

The words would not leave me. Why shouldn't I run? I drove home completely consumed with the idea. I wrestled with it for three weeks and realized that I wanted nothing else. I believe these years later that the Lord consumed me with the idea. Christine was opposed. I think I had already been a somewhat inattentive husband and father, and she thought she might lose me completely. I told her what I had come to realize, though: It was something I had to do. Once the idea entered my mind, I knew it was a path chosen for me. It was beyond me and beyond the moment. It was a calling.

Once I decided to run, there was only one thing I knew to do: get a book on managing a campaign. Fortunately, the Republican Party published one. I devoured it and followed it to the letter. I know this sounds silly, but it's the truth. Armed with knowledge of the process, I started touting the ideas that had been percolating in me since that Goldwater speech in 1964. I have never been the most dynamic speaker, but I think my principles fit the times. I talked about how Texas government had become a monster and how it needed to be tamed. I said I wanted to make the highway dollar worth a dollar, and advocated repealing the state sales tax and reforming property taxes, especially the estate tax. I mailed out twenty-six thousand well-aimed legislative questionnaires, and they raised both money and volunteers. People wanted change, and they were willing to work for it. The national mood was shifting. This was due in part to the education in conservatism that Ronald Reagan's nearly successful presidential campaign had given the country a year before, and to a growing weariness with liberalism, even of the more moderate Jimmy Carter variety.

I should not have won. I've said it long and often. It was a miracle to my supporters, an electoral oddity to my opponents. I received 13,012 of the nearly 24,000 votes cast, or 54 percent. And I became the first Republican elected to the Texas legislature in Fort Bend County since Reconstruction.

No one was more shocked than I was. Unless it was a rice farmer I had met during the campaign in front of Howard's cafeteria in Rosenberg, Texas. You could always tell the rice farmers because they wore a kind of uniform: brown cowboy boots, brown khaki pants, and a brown khaki shirt. This one must have been at least six and a half feet tall, and he was nearly three hundred pounds if he weighed an ounce.

I had learned to shake hands with Howard's customers *after* they ate. When they were going in, they were hungry and mean. Coming out, they had a moment. I approached this particular giant and said, "Hi, I'm Tom DeLay. I'm running for state representative. I'd like to talk to you about your vote." He looked down at me and said, "Now wait a minute. Wasn't that election about three weeks ago?" He was referring, of course, to the Democratic primary, the only one that had ever mattered in the area.

I said, "No, no, I'm the Republican in the race. My name is Tom DeLay, and I'm running for the general election in November."

Well, that did take him aback. He'd never seen a Republican before, and he had certainly never heard of me, one of the few idiots in Fort Bend County who would admit he was a Republican.

I waited him out, and finally he said, "I want to tell you something, boy. It'll be a cold day in hell when a Republican wins in this county."

Well, this rice farmer and I were both shocked on Election Day. And hell, which I suspect is somewhere near the Democratic national headquarters, probably was indeed a bit cooler that day.

All I knew for sure was that I had never worked so hard for a job that paid so little. By mandate of the Texas constitution a state legislator earns seventy-two hundred dollars a year. No wonder people think politicians are nuts.

Winston Churchill once wrote in his autobiography, *My Early Life,* that his conclusion about "Free Will and Predestination" was "that they are identical." He believed that as he made choices, he was fulfilling destiny, because man's choice is the vehicle of God's unfolding plan. This is very much how I see my life. I have chosen as I thought best. I chose to depart from my father's suffocating dreams, chose to work in pest control, chose to start my own business, and chose to run for the Texas legislature. I also chose Christine, the wisest decision of my life. Yet I am as sure as it is possible to be that all of this was according to a plan. Destiny ruled. Still, at that stage in my life, the grander plan had yet to be revealed. That plan would require a change in my soul that was still some years away. Thankfully, destiny did not let go of me in the meantime.

A MAN WITH NO CHEST

In C. S. Lewis's *The Abolition of Man,* his magnificent discourse on the power of moral education, there is a wonderful analogy of the head, the chest, and the stomach. Lewis suggests that if the head is the seat of reason and the stomach is the source of drive and appetite, then the chest—where the heart and soul are centered—is where character and morality reside. He doesn't mean this literally, of course. He is using these three as symbols to make a point, one that our generation desperately needs to understand.

Lewis says that we live in an age of "men without chests." We have intellect—the head. We have drive and ambition—the stomach. What we lack is character and morality. In a famous paragraph, Lewis wrote, "We make men without chests and expect of them virtue and enterprise. We laugh at honor and are shocked to find traitors in our midst. We castrate and bid the geldings be fruitful."

I must confess that as I began my career in politics, I was a man with no chest, to use Lewis's metaphor. I had the head because I certainly had ideas, and I was completely devoted to a conservative worldview. The stomach was working just fine, too. I was a man of passion, appetites, drive, and zeal. What I lacked was the kind of character that grows from a deep faith, the morality that comes from living for a spiritual purpose.

I would find my chest in time, and thank God I did. Until then, though, I was not the man I might have been. I gave in to my lesser appetites in my private life. Even in my political life, I lived out of a smallness of soul that made me hard to get along with, moved me toward the politics of anger, and left me an uninspiring figure. And in political leadership, as in all leadership, inspiration is everything. Thankfully, I learned from my mistakes, and God ultimately intervened. Still, it is sometimes hard to ponder my days as a man with no chest, and I do so both because I hope others will learn from me, and because I honor God by describing the dark side of my life with the same honesty that I describe the bright, shining moments.

The Texas legislature is an unusual animal. It is largely defined by the state constitution of 1876, which was written just as Reconstruction came to an end, and it was designed to make sure that no carpetbagger or scalawag—which meant Republicans from the North—could fashion a career in politics. This constitution sets the salary for a member of the Texas House of Representatives at a mere $7,200 a year. The legislature meets only six months every other year, with occasional special sessions. That's 140 days every two years, and clearly the purpose was, as a speaker of the Texas House once said, to make sure that it is hard to get legislation passed. It is. What's more, the whole system favors the wealthy man who wants to wield power rather than members of the middle class who have to earn a living while trying to make good laws for their beloved state.

I found it very difficult to run a business and serve in the Texas House at the same time. Though the job is supposed to be part-time, the districts have gotten so large that it has become a full-time job, and yet no one who isn't independently wealthy can live off of seventy-two hundred dollars a year. I believe, as I'll explain more fully later, that not paying elected representatives a living wage leads to only the wealthy running government, and to corruption. Being neither wealthy nor corrupt, I had to live off of my business, which I almost lost several times while serving in the House, and would have lost had Christine not stepped in brilliantly.

I started serving in the Texas House in 1979 as one of 32 Republicans out of 150 state representatives. My primary memory is of constantly being run over by the Democrats' political machine. The image of tire tracks up my back comes to mind. The conservatives in the House—both Republican and Democrat—used to call the section where the liberals sat "Red Square." They were extremists, and even the Democratic mainstream was suspicious of them. The speaker of the House was a Democrat named Billy Wayne Clayton, who ruled with an iron hand and a winning West Texas smile. He traded favors, bartered choice committee assignments, and glad-handed his way to astonishing power. He was also wise, though, and often appointed Republicans to committee chairmanships, something the citizens of Red Square would never have done.

Billy Wayne Clayton didn't like me, and there was good reason: I wasn't likable. I had come to the House with a bit of a chip on my shoulder. The truth is that I didn't like most of the people I served with, and it showed. I had decided to be a hard-ass. I voted no more than yes, kept myself aloof from the other members, and enjoyed my nonconformist, far-right conservative reputation. I was proud, I was prickly, and I was an idiot. The truth is, you don't get anything done behaving this way. Politics is the art of building coalitions, of winning people to your views, or at least of winning them to a spot as close to where you are standing as possible. I was the porcupine at the garden party, and no one was drawing near.

It was horrible in those early years. As I've said, I'm not the best speaker in the world. It takes me a while to organize my thoughts, and I'm better now than I was then. But it was sure bad then. When I spoke on the floor the Democrats used to chant, "Dee-lay, Dee-lay," an insulting reference to how long it took for my words to form. It didn't help that everyone in those days chewed tobacco in the House. I once got a bill to the floor, and then had to speak in defense of it, which meant the chaw of tobacco in my mouth lived there for nearly five hours without me spitting even once. This didn't exactly improve my oratorical skills.

Knowing that I was ineffective in those early years, I began paying attention to how the Democrats worked. For a long while I studied the process more than I studied the issues. I asked questions and tried to get the more successful Republicans to tell me how they got things done. It was quite an education and quite a rebuke to my arrogant, maverick style.

The first thing I noticed as I watched the Democrats was that they based their politics on personal relationships. This was more than just knowing the right people and knowing whose palms to grease. The more successful Democratic and Republican politicians tried to build good feeling even with their enemies. They knew how to tell a joke, how to talk about a man's interests, and how to keep political fights from getting personal. I was frankly horrible at all of this, and it was because, again, I hated these people. I thought they were in power to destroy my country, and I had no intention of giving them even an inch. I quickly realized that if I was going to get anything done in the House I had to change.

I watched Billy Wayne Clayton closely. Now when I first entered the House I thought he was a bumbling fool from West Texas. I couldn't believe someone like him had become speaker. Then I noticed that he knew how to handle people. He also knew the power of a favor. The day after he was elected to the speaker's chair, he would collect pledges to vote for him for speaker in the next session. These pledges would become the basis on which he would make committee assignments. He was always careful to make sure that the rules protected his position, and these rules guaranteed that the speaker could appoint half of the committee members. Clayton would load the important committee seats with his people, and then execute strategies at every level like a football coach calling in plays from the sidelines. This is how he grew power.

Then there were the lobbyists. When I first entered the House I thought most of these people were snakes. I intended to be above them. In time I realized that lobbyists represent issues and people I had sworn to serve. A lobbyist can be an important conduit of information and an important link to the institutions of society. You learned to know which ones kept their word and which didn't. You learned that character really was the issue, and that all of politics ran on whether a man had clear principles, kept his commitments, respected his fellow members, and rose above corruption. You also learned who had the courage of his convictions and who wouldn't stick his neck out for anything.

All of these observations worked themselves into a new political style for Tom DeLay. I would never be the archetype of the Southern, backslapping, Huey Long–type of politician. I was no Billy Wayne Clayton. I learned that I could gentle up, though. I could have a bit more respect and spend some time with an opponent socially to find some common ground. I soon learned that no one in the Texas House was evil, no matter how much I disagreed with him. I also saw that many members could be persuaded, that they were open to new information, and that they were impressed with you if you knew your stuff.

I can't say I set the world on fire because I was armed with this knowledge. My six years in the House were more of a learning time for me than they were a time of great legislative successes. My main achievement was in introducing the first deregulation of the trucking industry in twenty-five years. My goal was to lift restrictions on truckers that I knew would lower prices, increase competition, and improve service. It is pretty much the same thing I wanted to do to nearly every arena of government regulation in existence. I wanted to build a reputation for being a free market advocate for the simple reason that I strongly believe in the power of free markets.

The trucking lobby in Texas taught me a lot about political organization. They had battle groups at the local level. They wined and dined powerful people, and they even had a section of the gallery, which the members called "truckers' corner," where representatives of the industry glowered down upon the House members to make sure their bidding was done. Obviously, they weren't happy about my efforts. They stirred up their members in opposition to deregulation and launched a campaign of disinformation to stop me.

One day I was sitting in my tiny sophomore cubicle when two gigantic truckers walked up to my desk unannounced and they seemed very angry. They were the Guy brothers, and they operated an outfit called Guy Brothers Trucking. They had come to press the case of the trucking lobby, and they did more than hint that the argument might take a non-verbal form. Like many truckers, they had been riled up by their trade association, the Texas Motor Transportation Association (TMTA), which endorsed extremely intrusive regulation of the trucking industry. Sadly, the Guy brothers, like most of the TMTA's members, were never given a chance to understand what deregulation might mean for their business. Confronted by their hulking frames in my tiny office, I did the only thing I really could do: I started talking. I told them that if my legislation passed, a hauler wouldn't have to return from a haul empty just because some government regulation said so. I told them that my legislation meant that Guy Brothers Trucking could haul for anybody they wanted wherever they wanted throughout the entire state. I wanted to bring an end to the big trucking companies having their own little regions of overpriced shipping in which no one else could compete. The Guy brothers couldn't believe what I was saying. They hadn't been told the truth. When they left they shook my hand and told me they were for me. I was relieved, I can tell you, and began to suspect that some TMTA official was going to be the object of the anger originally intended for me!

It took me several years to change my reputation from a fire-breathing right-winger to a reasonable conservative that other members could work with. In partnership with some of the more left-leaning representatives, I sponsored legislation to make school lunches available to senior citizens, grant special parking permits to disabled persons, create a pilot program for parent education, and prohibit racial discrimination by the state's alcoholic beverage commission. Still, I held the line on some very controversial conservative principles. I refused to approve public education for the children of illegal aliens, resisted attempts to soften penalties for violent criminals, and tried desperately to lift costly regulations from the backs of business people.

Unfortunately, beyond the trucking bill, what people most remember from my time in the House is my partying. This is a much deserved reputation, and I can't fault my political opponents for keeping tales of my misdeeds in circulation. As part of Billy Wayne Clayton's efforts to build goodwill, he regularly hosted an event called "Spoke Night" at an old Austin dance hall called the Broken Spoke. It isn't hard to imagine the kind of place I'm talking about: low ceilings, red tablecloths, country-western music, and lots of chicken-fried steak. On these evenings representatives and lobbyists, reporters and bureaucrats mixed it up with each other and a battalion of adoring women, some of whom bedded politicians for sport. This is where I started going astray.

I was away from home for weeks at a time, I wasn't bad looking, and I got my share of female attention. In my first year, though, my problem wasn't women. It was alcohol. I got to the point where I was knocking back eight to twelve martinis a night and routinely getting home at two in the morning. I told myself I wasn't an alcoholic because, like my father, I could keep my drinking from interfering with my everyday life. If I wasn't an alcoholic, I was driving full speed down that road.

In my second session I roomed with five other guys, two Republicans and three Democrats. We called our town home "Macho Manor," which was more brag than fact, though we were bipartisan partiers and our place did become party central for a good number of politicians. Not much happened during the session that year. When my third session came around I roomed with my best friend, Gerry Geistweidt. We rented an apartment that had an old, shoddy hot tub. We dubbed our new place Hot Tub Haven, more as a joke than as a reality. Years later Beverly Carter of the *Fort Bend Star* newspaper picked up on the name Hot Tub Haven and began dubbing me Hot Tub Tom in her articles. The name stuck and came to symbolize all my excesses. I certainly deserved it. I drank too much. I slept with women I wasn't married to. I neglected my family. This is the truth, and I recount it with a deep sense of grief that I ever lived in such a manner.

The only redeeming truth from this period is that I did not allow my partying to interfere with my work, and this devotion is what moved me to set my sights on playing a greater role in shaping the nation. The defining moment came when my old nemesis, the Environmental Protection Agency, reared its head once again.

In 1978 the EPA decided after lengthy hearings to ban a chemical called Mirex, the best pesticide available for killing the imported fire ant. Now this critter is not the kind of fire ant you brush off your leg at picnics. This fire ant first arrived in the United States through Mobile, Alabama, after hitching a ride on steamships from South America. Though it is small, it secretes a powerful venom. If a cow gives birth to a calf on a bed of imported fire ants, the ants quickly kill that calf. These ants are aggressive, and they swarm. They are even powerful enough to kill large game birds. Sometimes when there are floods on the plains, basketball-sized nests of fire ants shoot down the rivers. The devastation to yards and crops is hard to exaggerate. Only one company made Mirex, and when the EPA banned its use that company went out of business. The imported fire ant was then able to do millions of dollars of damage throughout the southern portion of the United States.

I was livid. I had worked with Mirex for years, and I knew it was safe and effective when applied by somebody with experience. But here was the EPA—an unaccountable, unelected entity—again wiping out whole industries and banning products on the basis of bad science. It was infuriating and dangerous, symptomatic of what was taking place as the mythologies of the environmental movement held sway in our country. I decided that something needed to be done, and that I had as good a chance of doing it as anyone. As a biologist, I understood the issues. As a man with a six-year education in the Texas House, I had some feel for the mechanisms. As a businessman who could not seem to shake off the intrusion of government into his business, I had both the rage and the experience to strike, and to strike hard. So I decided it was time to run for the United States Congress.

I don't want to pass too quickly by my criticisms of the environmental movement. Given the statements I have made, I know that some will take me for an environment-raping, uninformed nut who must run his car overnight just to hurry the pace of global warming. Not at all. In fact, as a grandfather who loves the outdoors, if I thought for a minute that the EPA was genuinely doing what it claims to, I'd support it with everything I have. Unfortunately, the EPA has become a powerful instrument for environmental extremism. The agency is constantly seeking to expand its already overly broad regulatory powers to advance a left-wing environmental ideology that routinely and selectively ignores scientific fact and works hand in glove with left-wing groups that seem more bent on the destruction of capitalism than on the protection of the environment.

The environmental movement was virtually created in 1962 by Rachel Carson's antipesticide tome *Silent Spring*. Carson claimed that the human use of synthetic chemicals amounted to a "relentless war on life" and that modern society was "losing the right to be called civilized." I cannot take the time here to chronicle all of Rachel Carson's false statements, but suffice it to say that this lady was horribly misguided, her book as a work of science has been completely discredited, and her many errors have literally cost thousands if not millions of human lives.

Let's look at just one of her claims as an example. In 1948 a Swiss inventor by the name of Paul Hermann Müller won the Nobel Prize for inventing a pesticide called DDT, or dichloro-diphenyl-trichloroethane. The insecticide, developed in the 1930s, had already almost completely wiped out malaria in the developing world by the time Müller received his award. Unfortunately, with the publication of Carson's *Silent Spring*, DDT became the world's most vilified pesticide. It was abandoned immediately in most countries, and was banned completely in the United States in 1972. This despite the fact that in 1970, just two years before the ban, the National Academy of Sciences made this statement: "To only a few chemicals does man owe as great a debt as to DDT. In little more than two decades, DDT has prevented 500 million human deaths, due to malaria."

Now if DDT was as carcinogenic as Rachel Carson claimed, she would be right: Its use had to be stopped. It would be poised to murder millions, and a new method of halting malaria would have to be found. Tragically, Carson was wrong. Who says so? The United Nations World Health Organization. Late in 2006 the WHO reversed thirty years of policy and gave DDT a "clean bill of health." In fact, the WHO asked for environmental groups to support use of the pesticide in Africa to save the lives of babies dying of malaria by the millions.

Why did the WHO issue a call for the use of DDT in Africa? Consider the statistics. Worldwide an estimated 500 million people become sick from malaria each year, most of them in Africa, making the disease one of the greatest obstacles to economic development in the third world. In Uganda alone malaria costs more than $347 million a year. Forty percent of Uganda's outpatient care is devoted to treating malaria, and 80,000 people die of the disease each year, half of them children. Tragically, Africa accounts for 90 percent of the 2 million deaths from malaria each year.

Rachel Carson was wrong and people died as a result. In fact, she was so wrong that Dr. J. Gordon Edwards, a colleague of Carson's and a fellow environmentalist, traveled the country in the early 1990s trying to warn us of the dozens of errors in Carson's book. She was so wrong that the National Research Council, the research arm of the National Academy of Sciences, released a report in April 1996 that confirmed that many of the concerns Carson raised about carcinogens in food were unfounded. She was so wrong that third world countries are begging to use many of the very chemicals for which Carson tried to sound the death knell.

And Mirex, the chemical that kept imported fire ants under control? Well, after banning the chemical and closing the company that produced Mirex, EPA scientists years later concluded that it's not as bad as they had thought at first. It turns out that the EPA didn't do enough homework. Now not only is the company that once made Mirex out of business, but the EPA-mandated process to label Mirex again is too expensive to allow any company to bring it back on the market. Politics, not science, had prevailed. Again, if the EPA truly protected the environment, I would be its strongest supporter. It does not. Instead it has become a regulatory juggernaut fueled by flawed science, a socialist agenda, and sheer authoritarianism. It is easy for the left to depict Tom DeLay as an antienvironment nut, but children are dying by the hundreds of thousands because of the EPA's stupidity. When does that get addressed?

Still, I have the EPA to thank for one thing: I was so infuriated by their high-handed banning of a helpful substance, wisdom and compassion to the contrary, that my anger became the determining factor in a decision to run for Congress. There were other factors, of course. It was hard to make a living straddling both business and the Texas statehouse. Christine finally said that I should either get out of politics or get in enough to make a living. She insisted that we couldn't continue like we were. I agreed. I also knew that during my years in the Texas House I had honed a gift for the systems of government. I knew I could make a contribution to our country, and at a time when Ronald Reagan was undoing the liberal legacy of decades. If the Gipper was going to restore our "city upon a hill," I wanted to help him.

The moment that I best remember from the start of my campaign still brings a smile. I was called out to do a termite inspection for a couple who were both schoolteachers. The husband came home first to let me into the house, and when the wife came home later and joined us in the kitchen, I had my head under the sink with my butt up in the air looking for pests. The wife started explaining that she was late getting home because she had been doing some work for Tom DeLay's new campaign for Congress. At that moment I emerged dramatically from under the sink attired, of course, in my "bug suit," the coveralls I wore when I did an inspection. I introduced myself. It didn't work. They didn't believe me. A bit embarrassed but knowing all this was going to lead to a good laugh, I went to my truck to get my brochures and prove that I was indeed Tom DeLay. Once they were convinced I was able to thank these two teachers both for their support and for their business.

In the Republican primary, I had five opponents. It was quite a fight. One of them was named J. C. Helms, and he decided to make a big issue of some tax problems I had endured. The exterminating business is seasonal. You make a great deal of money in the spring and summer, but things slack off severely in the fall and winter. That's when the owner of a pest-control company has a choice: Lay people off and pay your taxes, or pay your people and let the taxes float. You usually can't do both in the winter months. I chose to take care of my employees. Christine could have killed me. She was right, and I had been softhearted and stupid. By the time that primary came around Helms was able to tell the public that the IRS had filed liens against Tom DeLay and Albo Pest Control in 1979, 1980, and 1983. He also declared that since I drove a red El Dorado Cadillac it was obvious I intended to ride it to Congress on the backs of the taxpayers.

Here is a classic case of a dictum popularized by Twain that there are three kinds of lies: lies, damn lies, and statistics. I had done what I thought was the compassionate, people-oriented thing to do, and yet I was vilified for being a tax evader and a deadbeat. Of course I had paid my taxes, and of course my record with the IRS was clear. Helms knew this, but it sounded better to paint me as a man using politics to escape his real-world responsibilities. I fought back. Helms held a press conference and I peppered the crowd with some sympathetic journalists. When the time came for questions one journalist asked Helms if that black

Cadillac in the parking lot belonged to him. He said yes. Then the journalist asked if Helms himself didn't owe back taxes, and wasn't it hypocritical to accuse DeLay when DeLay's tax problems had been cleared up, short term, and due to the challenges of managing a seasonal business. The candidate gulped, said yes, and that was the end of J. C. Helms. I ended up winning a six-way primary without a runoff, though I didn't get the news until three in the morning on the night of the election.

The general election was a formality since the district over the years had become very Republican. I was sure that election was going to turn my way when my Democratic opponent's stepmother told me that she had voted for me. It didn't hurt me either that Ronald Reagan carried Texas with 69 percent of the vote. By the grace of God, the work of a good campaign staff, and the gravitational pull of Reagan's presidency, I was elected to Congress as part of the largest class of Texas Republicans since the rigged elections of Reconstruction. It was the beginning of a true revolution, and I was grateful to be present at the creation of it.

What I needed was a true revolution in my personal life as well. I suppose this would not have been obvious to most of the folks who voted for me. I was thirty-seven years old, and I had just been elected to the United States House of Representatives. I had a moderately successful business, a beautiful and gifted wife, and a twelve-year-old daughter, Dani, who I'll describe more in pages to come. Moreover, I was being given the privilege of joining what would prove to be one of the most crucial ideological revolutions in American political history.

Yet the evidence confirms that there was something deeply wrong in my life. I was still drinking heavily, and I would continue to do so into the first few months of my congressional career. I had not stopped carousing, either. There were still women in my life, and this was despite the fact that Christine was the love of my life and I had a sweet daughter needing her father at home. Though I believed deeply in traditional values and defended them politically, I had abandoned traditional values as a guide to my personal conduct and ethics.

People often try to describe a man in such a condition as psychologically tortured or deeply disturbed mentally or emotionally. I won't deny this may be what leads some people into trouble. I tend to believe that more often the source of trouble is merely pride and rebellion. We know what to do but we choose not to do it. We enjoy sin. Even the Bible says that sin is pleasant for a season, and some of us spend a good deal of our lives moving from sin to sin, enjoying pleasurable seasons until the fun runs out, and we reach for a new high.

What amazes me as I look back on these years is how I was gravitating toward my father's horrible example and didn't realize it. True, I wasn't as controlling or bombastic as he was, but I was nevertheless dousing my life with alcohol and torturing a family with the overflow. I had my father's ability to divide myself, to maintain appearances, and to rationalize. In short, I had become a self-centered jerk. I'm still astounded by the ability I had to become what I abhorred. I guess this is coded into human nature, but it is a truly scary thing.

As I stepped onto the national stage then, I was eager to do good in the world, but I know now that the values I held were not connected to a spiritual bedrock in my life. I had a worldview but no relationship with the One who rules the world; I had truths but no grasp on the Truth. All of this would come in time and, when it did, I would finally start being the man I needed to be. Until then I would live out the famous words of St. Augustine: "Lord, you have formed us for yourself, and our hearts are restless until they find their rest in you."

COME THE REVOLUTION

In 1984 I joined a revolution—a revolution that would not achieve complete victory until 1994. Yet like most revolutions, it had to be fought first in the minds and hearts of men. It had to prove its ideas in the fires of debate and move men to action by replacing old excuses with a new call to arms. But the victory came, and when it did it changed America forever.

Most Americans think it happened long before it actually did. In 1984 Ronald Reagan defeated Walter Mondale in one of the greatest political victories in American history. Reagan won with 59 percent of the popular vote and 525 electoral votes, to Mondale's 41 percent and 13 electoral votes. It was an astonishing achievement, and by the oldest man ever to win the presidency.

People naturally assume that Reagan's victory changed the balance of power in the House and the Senate, but this is not what happened. The truth is that the GOP picked up only 14 seats in a House that had 269 Democrats and 166 Republicans prior to the election. In the Senate Republicans actually lost two votes, which made it the worst same-party performance in a reelection year since 1940, when Franklin Roosevelt won reelection over Wendell Willkie.

The Reagan revolution was definitely under way, but it had yet to claim victory in the halls of Congress. Its day would come, though, and I would have the privilege of helping to bring that day about. In the ten years leading up to the Republican revolution of 1994 I would help engineer the procedural and ideological changes that would ultimately mean victory for the values I held dear. Before I could play my part in these grand events, though, I would first have to undergo a revolution of my own.

The average American would probably be shocked to learn what a freshman congressman goes through when he first comes to Washington, D.C. For months prior to arriving that congressman has been worked to death in what was almost certainly the hardest fight of his life. It looks sexy in the press, though. There are pictures of the candidate standing next to famous people or getting on a private plane. Perhaps there is a cigar or a martini in his hand, and he looks like he is living it up, riding the ego train to the seat of power.

The truth is, he is exhausted. Unless he has an exceptional wife there are tensions in his marriage because of the pace and the strain on the family. His business—the law firm or the bottling company or the family car dealership that brought him to public attention in the first place—is probably suffering. He is in debt up to his eyeballs, and he can't remember the last time he had a quiet drink and a meaningful chat with a friend. That's all before he comes to Washington. Upon arriving he discovers that his learning curve is overwhelming, and that he has just stepped into the *Matrix:* Nothing will ever be as it seems.

Some congressmen never recover from this swirl. They learn to ride the whirlwind schedule and get things done, but rarely are they ever at peace, centered, or focused. In fact, rarely are they at their best. Adding to this hidden crisis is that they will be in constant need of money and they will live under the pressure of special interests, the temptation to drink too much, overeat, philander, and spend beyond their means will be more than most of them will be able to resist.

There is a better way, of course, and I tried to help create it, as I'll share in time, but my own awakening to the strangeness of Planet Washington came when I tried to buy a place to live. In Texas we had owned a ranch home that had a barn and so much land that we could keep horses. It wasn't anything special by Texas standards, but it was spacious and more than enough for us. Later we sold this ranch house and built another beautiful home that would probably be typical of middle- or upper-middle-class living in America. Again, it was nothing extravagant by Texas standards. When we moved to Washington, though, we ended up buying a tin box of a tract home that was twenty-five years old. It was astonishingly expensive even though it was actually just below average for the area. To make matters worse, our home in Sugar Land did not sell for ten months because Houston was going through its famous 1980s depression. We were saddled with two house payments for almost our entire first year in Washington, and it nearly wiped us out financially. I was only beginning to understand how stressful our transition was going to be.

It was even worse for Christine. We drove our two cars from Sugar Land to Washington, communicating on walkie-talkies the whole way so that Christine wouldn't get lost. She did anyway. The first time was just thirty minutes away from home! When we finally got to our new house in the nation's capital, Christine initially refused to drive to the grocery store for fear of getting lost again. I did all the grocery shopping in those first months, until I finally insisted that she learn how to drive the mile to and from the nearest grocery store. She mastered it—barely—but budgeted time for getting lost each time she went.

As if she and Dani didn't have enough stress already, I had stupidly agreed to allow PBS's *Frontline* to film us as part of a story on new congressmen settling into Washington life. I couldn't have made a move better designed to increase Christine's misery and Dani's humiliation. It was horrible. They filmed us from election night until committee assignments were made, and captured the whole process of winning, moving, choosing a new house, coaxing a twelve-year-old who did not want to move to behave for the cameras, and learning how to drive in Washington—badly. The producers even insisted that we buy a real Christmas tree, something we had never done before, and Christine had to sort through some two hundred boxes to find our Christmas ornaments so the nice PBS producers would be happy. It has been more than twenty years since that whole affair, and I think I have only recently been forgiven.

I came to Congress in 1984 as part of the largest Republican delegation in the freshman class. The six of us from Texas, which included Dick Armey, who was also elected that year, were called the "Texas Six-Pack." I told a journalist not long after I arrived that we were part of the "new young right." This was true, and though we probably could not have known it at the time, we were stepping onto a stage perfectly prepared for the new young right to make its mark on history.

The fact is that in 1984 House Republicans were only beginning to wake up from a half century of slumber. People said in those days that the Democrats had held power in the House for the thirty years since 1954. In reality the Democrats had seized the levers of government in 1930 at the dawn of the Great Depression and held it for the following five decades—through the New Deal, Truman's Fair Deal, the civil rights era, Lyndon Johnson's Great Society, and the deeply liberal and reactionary Watergate class of 1974. Only twice had the Republicans held the House during those five decades, and then for a total of only four years—once in 1946 during the Truman years, and once in 1952 on the coattails of Dwight Eisenhower. So insecure had those Republicans been that even when they held the majority they didn't dare move into the offices traditionally reserved for the dominant party. They kept their minority offices, fearful, I'm sure, that their victory would not be long lived. And it wasn't.

By 1984 Republicans had a serious inferiority complex, and there was no better symbol for this syndrome than Bob Michel, the minority leader. He was the epitome of what was wrong with Republicans, who had largely given up in the 1970s after the Nixon scandals and Watergate. Michel seemed content with the crumbs from the Democrats' table. His approach was known as "go along to get along," and his only strategy seemed to involve making friends with the Democrats on the Appropriations Committee in order to get the juicy projects necessary to impress the folks back home. I remember frequently hearing Michel comment in his speeches that not one Republican who had served during his time in Congress had ever been part of a majority. He said this as though it belonged in the *Guinness Book of World Records*. It was a losing comment made by a losing leader at the head of a losing party.

Most of the old Republicans I encountered in Congress when I arrived reminded me of what I'd heard about communists in Europe. They would sit around in coffeehouses and talk about what would happen "come the revolution," but never do anything to make a revolution happen. This is exactly what the Republicans did. They sat around and talked. They hoped that the force of their ideas would win the day. Crap. Ideas alone win nothing. What wins is an idea strategically set in motion. Republicans seemed to have forgotten that in 1984, so there were hours of meetings all over Washington in which Republicans moaned and discussed without much ever happening.

Then came Newt Gingrich. He was elected in 1978, and not long after began talking about what the Republicans might ultimately accomplish. The Republican leadership considered him, in their words, "a pain in the ass," but he got things moving. He was a former history professor with a doctorate in European history from Tulane and had been raised as a military brat on bases in Europe and throughout the United States, and he had done a thorough study of Margaret Thatcher's amazing political victories in England. Newt had a firm grasp on the ideas, but he understood what the senior Republicans did not: Ideas have to be married to action. He founded the Conservative Opportunity Society (COS), a group of young Republicans like Vin Weber of Minnesota and Bob Walker of Pennsylvania, who were committed to a conservative agenda and willing to cause trouble to bring that agenda about. The leadership called them "Gingrich's Guerrillas."

Much of what motivated these young turks was a capacity for outrage that the older Republicans seemed to lack. There were the ideological differences between Republicans and Democrats, of course, but there was also a high-handedness about the way the Democrats ran the House that seemed to incense Gingrich's gang, while creating only a slight stir among the older party leadership. In October 1987, for example, then speaker Jim Wright, a Democrat from Texas, rammed a budget bill through the House in a way that still lives in American political infamy. The procedural vote on the bill had been defeated because many conservative Democrats had voted against the $9 billion in new welfare spending called for in the bill. Wright then removed the welfare spending and brought the bill back to the floor for a vote on the same day it was defeated, something he could not do according to the rules without a two-thirds vote. To get around this Wright adjourned the House and then called it to session again, technically creating a new legislative day only twenty minutes later. He then sent for a fellow Texas congressman, Jim Chapman, and ordered the man to change his vote. Republicans still call the day of this underhandedness "Bloody

People have often commented about the smile on my face in the "mug shot" that the police took when I was indicted. I wish I could tell you that I felt nothing but peace. It wouldn't be true, though. . . .

I said a prayer and offered the best smile I could muster. All I wanted was for people to see Jesus in my life at that horrible moment. Thankfully, the picture my enemies wanted so desperately to be a sign of my downfall became instead a symbol of my new life. And, believe me, that new life has just begun!

I was born in Laredo, Texas, in 1947, just as the American lifestyle was creating a historic demand for petroleum. Our family would move to Venezuela a few years later so my father could put his expertise to use in the oil fields there.

My father, Charles DeLay, was loving and present in my early years. But by 1960, when this picture was taken with me in my Boy Scout uniform, he had turned to alcohol to cope with the death of his father and his life's other stresses. His alcoholism never seemed to affect his career, but it sure affected our family life.

"Christine," I wrote to my future wife on the back of this 1962 photo that she saved, "you're one of the nicest and sweetest girls that I've known. Love always, Tommy."

From the moment Christine Furrh asked me to the Sadie Hawkins dance I knew she'd be the love of my life forever.

We married on August 26, 1967. I worked in the athletic department's laundry room at the University of Houston while I finished college, and Christine worked in an insurance office. We were poor but in love.

In 1969 I graduated from the University of Houston with a degree in biology, and felt compelled to obey my father's wish for me to attend medical school. Christine reassured me that I didn't have to pursue a career I didn't want. I put my biology degree to good use in a pest-control business.

Three years later Dani was born. Here we are just coming home from the hospital.

Dani has been a great help to my career. In this photo she is helping me fix the headlights on my pest-control truck.

Dani and Christine were by my side the night I was first elected to Congress. It was 1984, and I went to Washington with the largest class of Texas Republicans since Reconstruction. I had joined a political revolution. But my personal life needed a revolution. I was drinking too much, I was away from home too often, and I was with women who were not my wife. One of Dr. James Dobson's films led me back to Jesus after too many years spent straying.

The Reagan revolution was definitely under way by the time I brought my family to Washington. (Here we are in 1987, in the Oval Office.) But it had yet to claim victory in the halls of Congress. That day would come, though, and I would have the privilege of helping to bring that day about.

I was elected House majority whip when the historic 104th Congress began in January 1995. Together with then speaker Newt Gingrich and then majority leader Dick Armey I helped bring the entire Contract with America to the House floor for a vote. But as time passed tensions arose between Gingrich and Armey and more conservative House Republicans dissatisfied with them. I was caught in the middle.

After the revolution's first two Congresses came to an end Newt decided not to run again for speaker and resigned his seat. I turned to my good friend Denny Hastert and told him, "Denny, you've got to be speaker." He turned white and protested, "No, no, no." The choice was obvious, though. Here we are with Christine at the speaker's rostrum.

Here I am with British prime minister Tony Blair when he visited Washington. It's important for politicians to travel abroad and exchange ideas, and in my opinion it's even better when taxpayers aren't footing the bill. I met with Margaret Thatcher and some British conservative activists when I visited England and Scotland—that's right, on the trip Jack Abramoff helped organize and a private foundation funded. And heck, yes, I seized the opportunity to play a round of golf at St. Andrew's while I was over there!

I think President Bush is a good man, and I wholeheartedly support his war effort in Iraq. But he has increased spending to historic levels and has done little to decrease the size of government. He may be compassionate, but he is certainly no conservative in the classic sense.

Thursday." The injustice of such tactics was not lost on Newt Gingrich, who complained loudly of how Democrats were "ruthlessly partisan in changing the rules of the House, stacking committees, apportioning staff and questioning the [Reagan] administration."

Newt did much more than complain, though. He knew how to strike back. He was particularly good at the art of television, and this is where he gave Tip O'Neill, an earlier speaker of the House, apoplectic fits. In 1979, during Gingrich's first year in Congress, O'Neill had engineered the decision to permit live, televised coverage of the House of Representatives. The speaker called it "one of the best decisions I ever made." He may have come to regret it. Newt quickly realized that he could reach more people by speaking before the new cameras in the House than he could by jumping on airplanes to make speeches to smaller crowds all over the country. He developed a strategy of bedeviling the Democrats with one-minute speeches before the cameras in the mornings, and then with much longer speeches, usually made before an empty House, in the afternoons. These afternoon speeches were called "special order" jabs, named for an order that entitled a member to take the floor after the House had finished its business and speak for an hour on any subject of his or her choosing. Though the House was usually empty, the speeches reached audiences watching from home.

Newt became the master of using this "special order" time. In fact, he began to fill the role, to use his words, of "politician as teacher." He would wander over to the floor in the afternoons and spend an hour skillfully teaching America the building blocks of a conservative worldview. Other members of the Conservative Opportunity Society followed suit. Some of them forced confrontations with the Democratic leadership before the cameras, hoping to expose the majority's lack of serious ideas. These tactics infuriated O'Neill. On May 10 of my first year one COS member's speech so angered O'Neill that he ordered the cameras to pan over the House floor to show that there was no one listening to the man. Several days later O'Neill exploded with rage at Gingrich and used such language that he was officially chastised on May 15. It was the first time since 1797 that a speaker was reproached because of his language, but it was confirmation that Gingrich's guerrilla tactics were working.

I had first encountered these new young Republicans at the 1984 convention in Dallas. They were impressive. They ran around doing their maverick thing before the television cameras, and at the same time they were skillfully executing strategies to influence the platform. I remember that they wore pancake makeup all the time because they never knew when they were going to be on television. I thought this was smart. All of us in the freshman class wanted to be like them. We were all Reagan babies, and we learned well the lessons that Gingrich and his gang had to teach. Know your stuff. Communicate well. Plan your work and work your plan. Action is everything. We can win this thing. These were the weapons in our arsenal and the slogans of our movement.

In my first term in Congress I knew I had an advantage over most of my fellow freshmen because of my years in the Texas House. I understood how the systems of power really work in a legislative body. Confident in my experience, I decided to set my goal high and shoot for a seat on the Appropriations Committee. Usually it takes a congressman three to five terms in office to land such an assignment, but I thought I could make it happen in two or three. It was worth the try. The Appropriations Committee is the place to be. Every bill that moves through Congress has to have funding approved by Appropriations. Without that funding, most acts of Congress are just hot air.

My plan was to try to get on the Committee on Committees first. This is where most of the committee assignments are made in Congress, and these assignments are everything. They determine status, power, and policy. The people who make those assignments make friends fast and have a profound impact on the system. Most freshmen would never know this. I had seen it before, though. I knew that by being the freshman representative on the Committee on Committees I would be at the table with senior leaders, I would be visible, and I could work for change within the system by making good assignments. I would also encourage the goodwill that would ultimately land me on the Appropriations Committee. My strategy worked. I gained the votes to get on the Committee on Committees, spent a year handing out plum assignments to others while taking horrible committee assignments myself, and in my second term I won a seat on the Appropriations Committee, where I could both serve my ideas and advance my career.

I know that what I am describing may appear to the inexperienced as a cynical grasp for personal power. It isn't. The reality is that when a man or woman sits in Congress they only serve their principles and their constituents well if they put themselves in positions to make things happen, to see their ideas become policy. This can be misunderstood as a naked grasp for position and, frankly, sometimes that is just what it is. Yet even the most altruistic member of Congress has to be positioned for power to see his ideas do any good. For too long Republicans had clung to their ideas and hoped that one day the nation would notice. No plan. No strategy. No action. It was folly. I had not come to Congress to play loyal opposition. I had come to see my ideas win, and seeking the choice assignments on the right committees was the way to take victory in hand. Anyone unwilling to position themselves for power in the service of their principles should stay out of politics.

I was busy then, during my first months in Congress, but unfortunately not too busy to continue my partying. I drank and drank heavily, knocking down my usual dozen martinis during an evening of revelry. There were also women and the same self-centered, pleasure-seeking ways that I had begun in the Texas House. Between my work and my fun

I did not seem to have time to meet with a senior member who kept asking for time with me. His name was Frank Wolf, a congressman from Virginia, and he never gave up trying to get me to agree to a time when he could drop by my office and talk to me. Thank God for his persistence.

I finally met with Frank six to nine months into my first term. We chatted for a while, and then he asked if he could show me a video called *Where Is Daddy?* It was a talk by Dr. James Dobson who was telling the story of how God convicted him for being away from home too much. Dobson then decided to leave his work as a lecturer and focus on his home life. This commitment and the video series that came from it became the launch of Dobson's immensely successful Focus on the Family ministry. None of this mattered to me at the time, though. I was in too much pain as I watched the video. Dobson said that most fathers are AWOL—Absent Without Leave—from their wives and their children. He said that studies revealed that the average father spends only 377 seconds with his children each day. I'll never forget some of Dr. Dobson's most damning sentences. He said, "Fathers have in their hands the power to save the family." And then there was his concern for the nation: "If America is going to make it . . . it will be because husbands and fathers begin to put their families first."

I am not ashamed to tell you that I wept like a child during that video. I was guilty of everything Dr. Dobson described. My daughter, Dani, was twelve as I sat there in that office, and I realized that I had missed almost her entire life through my self-centeredness and distraction. I remember that once when she was in the third grade she asked her mother "if someone had adopted Daddy," because I was never around. It was horrible to realize that I was destroying not only my family but, if Dr. Dobson was right, the moral fabric of the country I loved and yearned to serve. I saw as I sat there that I might have been a good conservative but I was not a good man. I might have been a successful politician but I was a failure at the most important job a man can have: loving his wife and child.

Frank knew that I was undone and told me that there was a Bible study group of members who were trying to work faith and family values into their lives. It was led by Tom Barrett, who was a gifted teacher and seemed to know what men like us needed. I told Frank that I would drop in, and then, in my fear and busyness, I didn't. Frank was again persistent, and he mentioned Bible study every time he saw me on the floor of the House. In time I began attending the weekly gathering. It became a conduit of life for me. Tom knew us better than we knew ourselves, and taught the Bible in a way that made it a blueprint for daily life. His words reached into my heart and into my situation in life. The transforming moment for me came one day during the meeting, when I quietly prayed a prayer of commitment to Jesus Christ. No one else was involved. In fact, no one else in the room even knew until later. I did it quietly, and yet with the greatest sincerity of my life. Finally I had made the commitment from my heart that I had long before made only with my words, as a teenager at Parkdale Baptist Church.

It is hard to describe the process of salvation to those who haven't experienced it. You simply have something new working around inside of you. People use different ways to describe it: There are new rooms in your inner house; there is a new Being speaking to you from the inside; you don't want what you used to want, and now you want new and holy things. All of this was true for me, but perhaps most of all there was a new hunger to drink in truth, and a new sense of love for God and others. My use of alcohol slowed dramatically. I repented of my ways with women, and have never gone back to that empty way of life. My heart turned fully to Christine and Dani, and they became the delights of my life. Most of all I had a passion to know and to please Jesus Christ.

I remember how the scriptures opened to me, and how everything we learned in the Bible study group affected me deeply. We dealt with ego, cultivating a servant heart, pride, ambition, managing our time, and how family comes first before our professions. These themes and others produced a dramatic turnaround in my life, and of a very practical kind.

The most dramatic area of behavioral change in my life concerned my family. Throughout the years I've been able to challenge dozens of incoming freshmen with the principles I learned in that Bible study group and began to apply. It starts with being honest. Congress is hard on families, particularly on wives. The government doesn't pay for spouses to travel to and from Washington, and so usually they are left at home. Then there are the challenges of maintaining two homes. Once a man lands in Congress he has two toothbrushes, two refrigerators, two beds—one in his hometown and one in Washington. The wife often feels like she has experienced a partial divorce: She's still married to the guy in his hometown, but he is also a single man with a whole other life in Washington. This does unbelievable damage to marriages. Then there is the stress and distraction of the schedule. Even when the man comes home, he is back in his district, and he is expected to tend to business. Women often complain that when their husbands come home at the end of the day, the body arrives in the house but the mind shows up some time later, or not at all. For the wives of congressmen returning to their districts, sometimes even the body never arrives. The men are home in name only.

Some men try to fix their wives' feelings by pledging undying love and sending flowers. It isn't enough. There have to be genuine, practical systems in place that position family first, and that build barriers to intrusions on family life. The policies I learned and put in place would be wise for every leader to employ.

First, involve your wife in all hiring. The truth is that the staff of a congressman, like most professional staffs, tends to view the spouse as an outsider, an interruption. This translates into the spouse being treated as a second-class citizen, which is not only wounding but dangerous, and may explain why so many affairs occur between executives and someone on their staff. The office or staff environment becomes a barrier against the spouse, and inappropriate affections often spring up behind those barriers.

Christine sat in on all interviews of new staff. I gave her veto power, so no one was hired without her approval. Not only did this give Christine peace about who I was working with, but it also sent a clear signal to the staff: "She outranks you. Don't screw with my family." Her phone call was always to be put through, and she was always to be given access to my work life. All staff knew this, and it made a huge difference.

Second, put a direct phone line in for your children. If you are going to be gone a great deal, let your children know they can always reach you. Give them a phone line that only you answer, and that you will answer no matter what is going on at the time. In our age of cell phones this gives your children instant access of a kind that few of their generation enjoy. Today there are even cell phones that allow the owner to answer several phone numbers. Dedicate one number to your children, and always answer that call. Let everyone in your work life know that a call from your children trumps all business.

I put just such a direct line in for Dani. She called it every day for a week. We had good talks each time, I told her I loved her, and then she never called it again. She didn't have to. Her heart had received the signal: "You are loved and you are my priority. I'm always here for you."

A third recommendation I made to congressmen was that they move their families to Washington. Most of the tensions and problems congressional families experience are easier to manage if the family is together and part of the congressman's life where the decisions are being made and most of the congressman's time is spent. I also recommended that the congressmen maintain a schedule for their weekends. Most congressmen spend their weekends making the rounds either in D.C. or back home in their districts. The family gets crowded out. I strongly urged the schedule that I learned from the men in our Bible study group. One weekend a month the congressman should be with his family, without exception. A second weekend should be spent in the district. A third should be spent at home, or as minimally in the district as possible. The final weekend should be spent in the district. On this schedule the family is guaranteed at least one weekend a month with the congressman at home, and they may get as many as two weekends. At the same time, the congressman is able to spend some time meeting with constituents and tending to the concerns of those he is sworn to represent. Having fixed schedules that make home life a priority like this are essential to a family's surviving a congressional career.

Finally, you have to keep your word to your family. If you don't make your word golden, if you don't teach your family to trust that you'll do what you say, then they not only lose respect for you, but they come to accept that there is no barrier to intrusions from the outside world. This leads to despair, bitterness, and, eventually, separation.

I broke this last principle for years, of course, when I was living the life of the selfish jerk. After giving my life to Jesus and starting to live a different set of values, I had the opportunity to prove my word to my daughter time and again. There was one occasion when she was playing in a seventh-grade band concert, and I agreed to go. Not long after telling her I would be there, I received a call from then vice president George H. W. Bush, asking me if I'd like to join him on Air Force One for the flight back to Houston. Now a congressman gets an offer like that once in a lifetime. Still, I had learned to live for a higher purpose than simply whatever moved me to the next rung of power. I declined and attended the concert. No, this doesn't make me some great fatherly hero. It just makes me a man who loves his daughter, and who has a lot to live down.

Over the years I urged many a congressman to put these strategies in place for the sake of their families. Every time I addressed an incoming class of freshmen and their wives I told my story and taught these steps. Some followed my lead and some didn't. I have had many husbands and wives come to me years later and say that either they put these ideas into practice and they saved their marriage, or that they wished they had because of the trouble they had known since. I understand only too well both stories, and constantly thank God that he rescued my family from my folly.

My newfound faith not only transformed my soul and my ethics; it transformed my vision for my nation. This was largely due to the influence of Christian men like Bill Bright and Charles Colson. I was so moved by their words, and by their emphasis on living out the meaning of 2 Chronicles 7:14, which reads, "If my people, who are called by My name, will humble themselves, and pray and seek My face, and turn from their wicked ways, then I will hear from heaven and will forgive their sin and heal their land" (New King James version). These two spiritual leaders spoke often about God's will for this nation, and of how prayer and repentance, combined with humble service, could turn the tide of spiritual decline the country has witnessed over the last century. They hoped and prayed for the healing of America. This convinced me. I had been a secular conservative/libertarian focused on limited government and fiscal responsibility. My faith transformed these values though, and made them part of a broader mission to restore the nation to the purposes of God.

I became a man with a renewed sense of mission. I read the Bible devotedly, and devoured every book that God put in front of me. I took courses on the Christian principles of the Constitution, and read some of the great works of American Christian history. I began to see how revivals had transformed U.S. culture, and how solemn gatherings for repentance and intercession had produced turning points in history. Hoping to see such powerful works of God spring up again, over the years I helped to sponsor a number of solemn ceremonies, as we called them, and was delighted to see both Democrats and Republicans on their knees before God. I helped launch several lecture series on Capitol Hill that included such solid men of faith as Roman Catholic scholar Michael Novak and conservative law professor Robert George. There were worship services for congressional families and staffers led by Christian artists like Michael W. Smith, and there were small groups devoted to studying everything from Rick Warren's *The Purpose-Driven Life* to biblical principles for transforming poverty.

I soon came to understand that there was a whole movement of people like me who had for years been crying out to God for their country. They wanted to see healing in their land. They wanted to see the age-old covenants renewed and righteousness restored. They believed that America had a unique mission in the world, and it wasn't to be the largest exporter of pornography and abortion on earth. It was to be a model of freedom and prosperity, of justice and holiness for the world. As I grew in my faith, I grew in understanding of who these people were, and I longed to help them heal my country.

Moved by my developing worldview, I began to talk more openly about matters of faith in my political speeches. I also began talking about the culture of our country as much as I spoke about limited government and balanced budgets. I was pleased by the response. The American people on both sides of the political spectrum were concerned about the spiritual decline of their country in a way I had not fully understood. This was the vein of concern that Ronald Reagan had tapped when he talked about America as a "city upon a hill," or about religion

as the bedrock of our institutions. In my run for reelection in 1986 I was a different man from the one who had first gone to Washington in 1984, but my constituents embraced me and sent me back to Congress with a 71 to 39 percent victory. I was never seriously challenged in my district again.

There is a principle of life and leadership that has often proven true in my life, and it is this: A man's gifts make a place for him. If you work at improving whatever it is you do well, your skill will eventually open doors. The truth of this principle led to one of the great turning points— and crises—of my career. I do not have many gifts, but my systems-oriented mind makes me good at what politicians call "counting the vote." This does not mean merely counting voters. It is a fairly laborious process of figuring out how members of Congress are likely to vote on a given issue and how that vote can be influenced. You have to ask the right questions: What is a given member's philosophy on the issue in question? How does this issue play in his district? Who is influencing him to vote as he does? What would need to happen for his vote to change in my direction? Counting the vote is a bit like projecting what teams are going to win in a tournament. You have to know enough about the players, the coaches, each team's history, and the strategy of the game so you can project who is going to win. This is what counting the vote is like in politics, except it often includes sitting down with a member to see how you can win him to your way of voting.

I had become pretty good at this in the Texas House, and I improved in my first couple of terms in Congress. By the 1988 Republican convention in New Orleans my gift for counting votes had come to the attention of then congressman Dick Cheney, who was soon to be the House minority whip. The term "whip" in politics comes from the Brit-

ish fox hunts in which there is a "whipper-in" who corrals the hunting dogs toward the fox. The British Parliament picked up this term and used it for the politician whose job it is to make sure all of the members of a certain political party attend meetings and vote as the party leadership decides. A whip, particularly one as astute as Dick Cheney, knows the value of a good vote counter, and at the New Orleans convention he decided to test my abilities.

Cheney wanted to pass a rule that had to do with floor privileges at the convention. The exact details aren't important, but suffice it to say that it was a hotly contested issue between the party bureaucrats and elected officials that had not been won by the elected officials in eighty years. Cheney told me to "whip the vote" for the rule change he wanted to pass. He knew it was a nearly impossible assignment. Still, I went to work and, miraculously, I got the votes. Then I decided to show off. I wrote down on a piece of paper exactly what I knew the vote count would be, and I handed it to Cheney. The vote came in exactly as I had written it. Cheney was impressed, the rule change passed, and I was thankful that a senior member was taking note of my gifts.

That's what got me in trouble not long afterward. Cheney began talking about my becoming chief deputy whip, a role I knew I could do well. I was eager, but I waited for the political wheels to turn my way. In the meantime, new president George H. W. Bush decided to appoint Texas Senator John Tower as the secretary of defense. The nomination should have gone through, because Tower was highly qualified, but in the poisoned atmosphere of Congress, the Senate Democrats decided to beat Tower up over spurious allegations of drinking, womanizing, and being too chummy with the arms industry. Tower was not confirmed, and Bush appointed Dick Cheney instead.

Immediately, the race for Cheney's minority whip position began.

Newt Gingrich later said that as soon as he heard the news of Cheney's nomination he knew he was going to run for minority whip. There were others eyeing the position as well, men like Henry Hyde. Minority leader Bob Michel's choice was Illinois representative Ed Madigan, who almost immediately asked me to manage his campaign for the position. I had a choice to make. I was definitely more aligned philosophically with the Gingrich crowd, but I frankly didn't think Newt would be a very good whip. I'll discuss his leadership style more in time, but though he is a great field general, he does not think strategically, and was about the worst vote counter I had ever seen. I honestly thought Ed was the better choice for the role. I also don't mind admitting that if Newt had won, I was going to be a minor whip in the party, but if Ed won I was going to be chief deputy whip, in a seat at the leadership table. Remember, political leadership is very much about positioning for power, and I freely admit that this was a factor in my thinking, as it should have been.

I decided to back Madigan, and the race was on. As hard as we worked, we lost by one vote. It happened at a conference breakfast, where Larry Coughlin from Pennsylvania was the deciding vote, and was supposed to vote with me. He switched at the last minute though, and backed Newt. I was forced to swallow my pride, because that same day Newt had to whip a vote, and I ended up in his office. Naturally he wasn't happy with me, but he was gracious nevertheless. I had to start from scratch, because the credit I had built up left with Cheney, and I had opposed the new whip. Still, from that day forward I set my sights on a new path. It would involve aligning with Newt on conservative values and no longer trying to curry favor with the old order.

There is no question that Gingrich was what we needed. He drove Bob Michel crazy with his activism and his attacks on the Democrats. The go along to get along Republicans grew increasingly nervous over Gingrich's

bomb throwing and accusations, but they probably also sensed that their days were numbered. There was a new sheriff in town, and he had no intention of satisfying himself with crumbs from the Democrats' table.

In fact, it was a confrontation with one particular old-line Republican that truly galvanized the younger, activist conservatives into a solid core. Though many of us had come to Congress as Reagan babies, we eventually found ourselves doing the bidding of his former vice president, George H. W. Bush. He was from the older, more moderate Rockefeller wing of the party, and we young conservatives sensed that he didn't truly share our values. Nowhere was this more evident than in his promise of "no new taxes." We loved this rallying cry and used it to urge support for Bush among our congressional colleagues. Then he abandoned it. A number of us had to nearly force our way into a breakfast meeting with Bush to tell him that he was in danger of losing reelection if he ignored conservative economic principles. He listened, thanked us, and walked out. He hadn't heard a word. We knew we were in trouble. The storm clouds were gathering, and Bush couldn't see them.

In the meantime I came into a position that not only allowed me to further the budding conservative revolution, but to rebuild my sagging political fortunes in the wake of the minority whip race. This was largely the doing of Ed Buckham, who was then the executive director of the Republican Study Committee (RSC). He urged me to become the RSC's chairman. I liked the idea. The role came with a dozen or so additional staffers, and allowed me to help shape Republican policy on major issues. Buckham became my champion, and started working up the votes to secure the job for me. In fact, he saved me. At a time when I was outside of Gingrich's inner core of activists, my RSC chairmanship put me in a visible leadership position, and gave me the defining role I longed for. I will always be grateful to Ed.

I ran the RSC like a shadow leadership team that was completely

separate from the Republican leadership. Bob Michel certainly did not care about what we were doing, and Gingrich was distracted by other matters. This gave me the freedom to develop the RSC as I thought best. I had been studying the systems in Congress for years, and I believed I had identified some strategies that could assure victories for conservative principles. In time these strategies would be absorbed by the broader Republican leadership, and would eventually help us win the majority in 1994.

First, we began to realize that it only took five or six members to push an initiative through Congress. This led me to develop action teams composed of five or six members who were committed to each other for a specific course of action. We would pick three or four issues, form an action team to champion each one, and then the teams would meet for thirty minutes each week to execute a defined strategy. I would not let these teams talk about policy. Republicans had spent years talking policy to no avail, and we were long past that need. We desperately needed to act, so I insisted that each team meeting remain brief, focused, and execution-oriented. This approach to change was hugely successful. In fact, I believe this small-team, action-oriented strategy allowed us to defeat Bush's first attempt to raise taxes contrary to his campaign promise. This was a huge victory for us, and it modeled an approach to change that was soon employed throughout the party.

Second, we committed to fashioning an alternative to every bill or amendment the Democrats proposed. Rather than develop our ideas in the abstract, we sent them into battle in direct opposition to every major liberal initiative. This proved to be an effective strategy. First, it put the Democrats on notice that we intended serious ideological warfare. Second, it focused our thinking around specific issues and helped us hone our ideas as we answered each principle of liberalism. Third, it illustrated to the American people that they had a choice. It told them that there really were wise alternatives to liberal folly, and that there was a well-oiled machine in place to execute these alternatives. In other words, it told the people that they had a choice and not an echo. This strategy of meeting every Democrat initiative with a conservative answer would ultimately lead to the Contract with America.

Unfortunately, these strategies were being implemented behind the scenes while a disaster was unfolding before the watching world. In the election of 1992 George H. W. Bush lost the presidency to Bill Clinton. The incumbent president won only 37 percent of the vote, down 16 points and nearly 9 million votes from four years earlier. It was an astonishing defeat that left the party in shambles. Major Garrett's insightful book *The Enduring Revolution: The Inside Story of the Republican Ascendancy and Why It Will Continue* contains a summary of the horrible Republican situation by the early 1990s. It was written by GOP strategist Don Fierce, and it captures, with humor and brevity, where we were:

> Reagan picked up Democrats in the 1980s. They got in his pickup truck and they rode with him for eight years. Then Bush comes along in his Volvo. They won't get in. But then he promises not to raise taxes and they get in the Volvo and ride with him until he raises taxes. Then they get out and they are pissed. . . . We did not have a leader. We didn't have a president. Republicans weren't going to listen to Dole, and precinct Republicans didn't know enough about Gingrich.

The truth is that the Republican faithful felt betrayed by Bush's reversal on taxes, and had lost their zeal for the party. When Bill Paxon became head of the National Republican Campaign Committee in 1993, he discovered that it was broke. He cut staff from ninety-three to twenty-six just as banks started calling in notes. Fund-raising had dropped off, due to the thorough disillusionment of the base, putting the committee in crisis. Serious-minded people began discussing the possibility that the National Republican Campaign Committee might become the first party committee in Washington history to close.

The Republicans were in crisis, but of the kind that often summons greatness from men and movements. True, there was much smallness and clinging to position. As former Iowa congressman Fred Grandy— who played Gopher on the 1970s series *The Love Boat*—once said, "The trouble with Republicans is, they don't have anything and they won't share." This was too often the case, but some good leaders did arise during this season of crisis, and they did save the party. Our political opponents helped us more than we ever thought they would.

What soon formed was the perfect storm of Republican resurrection and Democratic folly:

- New Republican Party chairman Haley Barbour wisely refashioned the party to make it more high-tech, better connected to state parties and small donors, and more a party of ideas. He also mailed out more than four hundred thousand surveys to get a better sense of what the average Republican was thinking. Overwhelmingly, the party faithful were committed to core conservative values: smaller government, balanced budgets, lower taxes, welfare reform, increased defense spending, reform of Congress, and fewer federal regulations. In other words, they wanted the party of Reagan and not Bush, of Goldwater and not Rockefeller. Newt and his young radicals got the message.
- Bill Clinton started strong but stumbled quickly. He and his wife, Hillary, bungled their attempts to institute a universal health care plan and distanced many Americans by supporting gays in the military. These efforts and a proposed budget that looked like liberal

tax-and-spend economics run amok scared conservatives nationwide and launched them into action.

- Newt pulled his core leadership team together and began talking
  about nationalizing the race. In meetings that included Newt, Bill
  Paxon, Bob Walker, Dick Armey, and me we began to hammer out
  the strategies of the revolution, incorporating many of the tactics I
  had developed as chairman of the Republican Study Committee.

- Understanding that money is the mother's milk of politics, we raised
  huge sums from a voter base afraid of the Clintons, and began pouring support into vital races around the country. This shocked the
  old guard, who thought the practice of nationalizing fund-raising
  was somehow "unsporting." We argued that it was just such atti-
  tudes that had kept us in the minority, and that it was time for a new
  approach to fund-raising, one that was national and values-oriented
  rather than local and limited to a single campaign. Dick Armey and
  I approached donors and built nationwide networks of fund-raisers,
  while Newt used his media savvy to refill Republican war chests.

- In October 1993, House minority leader Bob Michel announced his
  retirement, signaling that the "old bulls" of the Republican Party
  were letting go of the controls.

- Evangelical Christians offended by Clinton's support for gays in the
  military and abortion on demand mobilized in huge numbers. In the
  2 weeks before the 1994 election the Christian Coalition distributed
  33 million voter guides. Religious conservatives ended up comprising
  35 percent of the vote, a 10 percent increase over 2 years earlier.

Our strategies worked. When Election Day came the results were
astonishing. For the first time in forty years Republicans took control of
the House, having won 52 seats to claim a 230 to 204 majority. Not one
incumbent Republican lost his election. Republicans also won the Sen-

ate 53 to 47, assuming a majority for the first time in 8 years. The revolution had finally come, and victory was indeed sweet.

There was a moment that I find particularly meaningful all these years later. After Newt Gingrich was elected the new speaker of the House, and the day came for the passing of the gavel, outgoing speaker Dick Gephardt turned to Newt during the ceremony and said, "With resignation but with resolve, I hereby end forty years of Democratic rule of the House. You are now my speaker. Let the great debate begin."

And so it did, but while I do not know exactly what Gephardt meant, I do know now the nature of the debates that began that day. They were debates between conservative and liberal policies to be sure, but they were also more. They were debates about honesty and the kind of character that deserves to exercise power. They were debates about whether the God who created this nation should be honored in its institutions. They were also debates about whether political opponents should be defeated by a vote or destroyed by a court. And they were debates about whether America is a land of exceptional calling and purpose that ought to be protected at all costs. These were the debates we were about to face, but in that heady moment of our glorious victory, we could not have foreseen the cost of the battles to come. Perhaps it is best we could not.

IN THE INTEREST OF LIBERTY

The British writer G. K. Chesterton once wrote, "Christianity has not been tried and found wanting; it has been found difficult and not tried." I think the same is true of conservatism. It is seldom tried but often dismissed as unworkable in our modern age.

Part of the problem is that leading Republicans frequently get credit for being conservatives even when their policies are the furthest thing from conservative. Then, when their policies fail, the press presents the resulting mess as a failure of conservative principles. Richard Nixon, for example, gladly welcomed the conservative label, but his economic policies and expansion of government were closer to socialism than classical conservatism. George W. Bush calls himself a "compassionate conservative," but he has expanded government to suit his purpose, especially in the area of education. He may be compassionate, but he is certainly no conservative in the classic sense.

I have tried throughout my political life to maintain a rigorous devotion to conservative principles. This has won me the hatred of liberals and the irritation of less conservative Republicans, but from the time I entered politics I have fought for certain clear principles that I think are the principles of freedom: small government; low taxes; the rule of

law; an unrestrained free market; protection of private property; a strong defense; and traditional family values. These are what I believe in, and these are the principles that have been my guide. In fact, I have been devoted to these truths ever since my conservative epiphany during the Goldwater speech of 1964.

Goldwater also influenced many of my generation with a more systematic statement of conservatism called *The Conscience of a Conservative,* a brilliant little book that has sold over 3.5 million copies since it first appeared in 1960. Among its jewels is one paragraph in particular that summarizes well what I attempted to do in Congress, and I include it here because it is impossible to understand who I was as the majority whip and the House majority leader from 1994 until 2006 without understanding the principles I attempted to serve. Goldwater wrote:

I have little interest in streamlining government or in making it more efficient, for I mean to reduce its size. I do not undertake to promote welfare, for I propose to extend freedom. My aim is not to pass laws, but to repeal them. It is not to inaugurate new programs, but to cancel old ones. . . . I will not attempt to discover whether legislation is "needed" before I have first determined whether it is constitutionally permissible.

This is true conservatism. This is, as I understand it, the politics of order, justice, and freedom. This is what I attempted to accomplish as a leader in the Republican majority—to serve, in Goldwater's phrase, the interests of liberty.

It was Harry Truman who once quipped in a moment of frustration, "If you want a friend in Washington, get a dog." I understand the feeling,

but as Republicans took the reins of power in 1995 I was fortunate to have a friend in Washington named Dennis Hastert. He made a tremendous difference in my life at the time, just as he would make a difference in the life of the nation some years later. Few, though, knew who he was in 1995. He had come to Congress in 1986 after sixteen years of coaching and teaching high school and six years in the Illinois House of Representatives. He was so beloved in his home state and in the world of wrestling that he was awarded the National Wrestling Hall of Fame's Order of Merit. I grew to love him because he was a gentle giant of a man, with the kind of intelligence, character, and political wisdom that I found to be rare in Washington. And in 1995, I needed him.

When we took the majority there was little question that Newt Gingrich was going to be speaker of the House, and there was little question that Dick Armey was going to be the House majority leader. These races held no drama, since both men ran unopposed. I had come to believe that I could serve the country and advance my principles best by running for majority whip. I knew I had the skills, and I also thought I saw ways to improve the whip operations I had seen. The problem was that Gingrich's choice for whip was Bob Walker, who had been one of the founding members of the Conservative Opportunity Society. Walker had been Newt's pit bull on the floor, harassing Democrats and sharing the C-SPAN special order limelight. The two of them had become close friends and were definitely at the core of the inner circle, while I was barely at the outer edge.

I thought I had two advantages, though. First, I knew I could do a better job at whip than Walker because I was simply better at counting and working votes than he was. Second, I was better known among the incoming freshman class because of my work in their campaigns. During that harried election season I had traveled to twenty-five states in support of candidates, and had developed fund-raising networks that covered every state in the nation. To help the Republicans achieve victory, I had even run a candidate school that got down to such details as talking points and yard signs. I personally worked with and supported some eighty candidates, and by the time seventy of them entered the freshman class, I had commitments from fifty-three to support me for Republican whip.

I also had Denny Hastert. He agreed to manage my campaign for whip, and he was brilliant. He put together a twenty-member team to work the House Republican conference, and he partnered with Mildred Webber, a consultant who had helped me with my fund-raising work in all those congressional races.

It was thrilling to be running for a position I knew I could do well, but it was also nerve-racking to be opposing Newt again, particularly now that he was in the most powerful position in the House of Representatives. Oddly, he didn't come out strongly for Walker. And Denny did such a great job managing my campaign, and I was so well known for my work among the new members, that we won. I got 119 of the votes to Walker's 80, which left 28 for Florida representative Bill McCollum, who had also decided to run. In gratitude, and in recognition of his skill, I immediately appointed Denny as chief deputy whip.

Following the race I said something I later regretted. I was asked why I thought Newt hadn't backed Walker as strongly as many expected, and I said, "He knew I would make a terrible enemy." This was me speaking from the dark side of Tom DeLay. We are all flawed, and my flaw is that I can sometimes be aggressive, even mean. Christine warns me constantly about this. She says I can't say the word "judge" without saying "activist judge," and that I think "stupid liberal" is one word. She is right. Though I ask God for help, I do sometimes work from an anger in my soul that I first felt in the Texas House when I saw liberals as enemies trying to destroy my country. Even in an all-Republican race I can get so geared up for war that I speak of my allies as enemies. This is where Denny Hastert has been a great friend over the years. He keeps a rein on my aggressiveness and helps me see the larger view. He is a model of big-heartedness, and I have become a better man through his influence.

Once I won the majority whip position, I was eager to get to work. I had been studying the way a vote was usually whipped in Congress, and I thought there was a better approach. Normally party leaders waited until a vote was scheduled for the floor of the House, and then they did a "whip check," which means they began talking to members to see how each one would vote. This was usually only a week or so before the vote took place, and it didn't leave enough time to make sure everyone's concerns were answered so that the vote would go our way. I didn't see any reason for the uncertainty. I decided that it was possible to put an organized whip operation in place from the moment the bill was introduced. By dividing members into teams and working the vote systematically from the beginning, you had time to find out how each member planned to vote, what might win over those who were uncertain, and what amendments might be attached to your bill to compel members' votes. You could fight out problems with the leadership and negotiate the compromises needed to make the vote successful. By the time the bill made it to the floor members were eager to vote for it, because their concerns had been answered. This approach was harder work than the traditional way of whipping a vote, but it ultimately led to greater success for our policies. We came to call this strategy "grow the vote," and it was a revolutionary innovation that gave us victory after victory.

Another strategy I thought could help us was to start every policy initiative from as far to the political right as we could. We knew that the Senate, and certainly Bill Clinton, would pull the issue to the center— that they would try to soften our conservative positions—so we decided to move the center farther to the right by starting the whole debate from a far-right position to begin with. For example, if there was a spending bill under consideration we would propose spending that was drastically low, because we were committed to cutting spending, and thus cutting the size of government. Clinton would naturally pull toward the left, and the Senate would always pull toward the middle. So the lower the numbers we used to start the discussion, the lower the compromise number would be, and the closer to conservative spending levels we would ultimately be. This strategy gave us a much greater success rate than we had ever known.

While I was launching these innovations within the machinery of our party, Newt was engineering a transformation of the House. From the first day on the job he signaled his intention to work hard and cut deep with a fourteen-and-a-half-hour marathon session. He dynamited the power of the old guard by choosing committee chairmen according to their ability and not their seniority. He also limited terms for committee chairmen to no more than three, meaning a six-year maximum, and cut committee staffs by a third. Numerous committees and subcommittees were eliminated, including Committees on the District of Columbia, Merchant Marine and fisheries, and Post Office and Civil Service. Newt even abolished the office of doorkeeper and transferred its functions to the sergeant at arms. His staff literally roamed the halls of Congress to learn who did what and how it all might be done more efficiently.

The most important success of those early days was in bringing the Contract with America to the floor. The idea of the contract had emerged during the election season, when Newt, Paxon, Armey, Walker, and I were meeting regularly to set strategies for nationalizing it. I honestly can't remember whose idea the contract was, but I believe Dick Armey first proposed it, I suggested an alternative, and Newt named it. I was strongly in favor, because it was an approach that paralleled what we

had been doing on the Republican Study Committee, in answering every major Democratic initiative with a Republican alternative. The idea of offering a specific Republican agenda to the American people appealed to many of our members, because we knew we had a credibility gap. Republicans of the go-along-to-get-along stripe had taught the country to expect little change from our leadership, and George H. W. Bush's reversal on taxes had damaged our credibility horribly, even with our own base. Many of our members sensed that the time had come to make a specific list of policies we would enact if voted into power. Our attitude would be, as we later proclaimed, "If we break this contract, throw us out. We mean it."

Many Americans can still remember the dramatic event on September 27, 1994, when 337 Republican House members and candidates gathered on the West Front of the U.S. Capitol to sign the contract. What many Americans do not know, though, is that the legislative language behind each principle of the contract was already written, before it was unveiled. In other words, we presented ten legislative commitments to the American people, and we had already written the legislation that would make these commitments a reality if we won the majority. It was a massive undertaking, one that I believe was as historic as the event on the Capitol steps. We were making a covenant with the American people that guaranteed:

1. A balanced budget amendment and a legislative line-item veto to restore fiscal responsibility to Congress
2. A strong anticrime bill that expanded the death penalty and required longer jail sentences for felons
3. A "personal responsibility act" that would reform welfare by forcing able-bodied recipients off public assistance after two years and reduce welfare spending

4. A "family reinforcement act" that would, among other things, provide tax incentives for adoption and establish an elderly dependent-care tax credit

5. A $500 per-child tax credit; a reduction of taxes on married couples; and the creation of tax-free savings accounts available to help families cover the cost of college tuition, first-time home purchases, or medical expenses

6. A strong national security defense bill that would protect defense spending from further cuts, eliminate any possible United Nations command of U.S. troops, and call for the swift development and deployment of a national ballistic missile defense system

7. A provision that seniors could earn more without losing their Social Security benefits

8. Eliminating federal unfunded mandates (that is, federal laws that require states or communities to take particular actions but do not provide the funds necessary for the actions) and passing other reforms to create new jobs and increase wages, such as reducing the capital gains tax and providing incentives for small businesses

9. A reduction in damages awarded in civil cases and other "common-sense legal reforms"

10. Term limits for senators and congressmen

It had been hard work creating the contract and then getting all the members of the Republican House conference to sign off on it. I have to give Dick Armey credit for much of this, because it was his job to pull the whole thing together, and he did it. Every Republican House member agreed to the contract except one, Don Young from Alaska. Other than this one holdout, the House members of the Republican Party were offering the nation a clear, reasoned agenda, and were inviting Ameri-

cans to give Republicans the boot if they broke their word. It was bold, it was risky, and it apparently worked as a campaign strategy. We won.

I agreed wholeheartedly with the entire contract except for the call for term limits. I could sign the contract even with this provision, because the contract was a commitment to bring specific legislation to the floor, not to guarantee it would become law. I agreed that term limits ought to be brought to a vote, and it was, but when the time came I voted against it. The reason I did is that I believe term limits violate the constitutional right of the people to choose their leaders. My whole conservative philosophy is built on the idea that the people should be free to choose without government mandate or restraint. Why should there be any limit on how long a representative can serve as long as a majority of his constituents still have confidence in him? Besides, any limit on the number of terms a representative can serve would have to be arbitrary. Who is to say that three terms is better than four for a congressman, or that five terms is better than six for a senator? Why can't the people choose for themselves? Does Congress know better than the people of a given state who ought to represent them and for how many terms? I say Congress has less wisdom than the people, and that is why I oppose limiting the people's choices. The bottom line for me is that we already have term limits in America. They are called elections.

My one concern aside, it was a privilege to help move the contract to the floor, and a privilege to be a part of the 104th Congress. We were making history, though you would not have known it by the way our achievements played in the press. Critics assailed us as all talk and no action. Even the *Congressional Quarterly* summarized the 104th Congress by saying, "Republicans scored very few achievements." This was because in the first one hundred days of the Congress only two bills were signed into law. Only one was signed into law in the second hundred

days. In fact, for the entire first year of the 104th Congress, only eighty-eight bills became law, the fewest passed in a session since 1933.

I wear these criticisms as a badge of honor. The truth is that we were attempting historic change. We were not just passing bills to pave a road or fund a new missile system. We were redefining the way America is governed and making fundamental changes in systems that had been erected over decades. It wasn't bound to be fast or easy, and we knew we would probably disappoint the Washington pundits who always seem to want immediate, statistically verifiable change to report in their articles. Instead we moved the whole of American governance to the right, and made changes that will shape our grandchildren's lives. We moved a liberal president to the center and drove him toward a balanced budget; welfare reform legislation of a far more conservative type than he had intended; and more spending on defense, though he had entered office planning to spend less. We redefined the national debate on gun control and abortion. We provided the basis for future tax cuts, urged reconsideration of the Strategic Defense Initiative, and applied conservative principles to a host of social programs in crisis. There is little doubt that our work in the 104th Congress shaped American political history for decades to come.

Much of what energized our revolution was our visceral opposition to Bill Clinton. I've gone back and read articles about me that describe my face flushing and the veins in my neck sticking out when his name is mentioned. It is all true. I openly admit that I just don't like the man, and my disgust is both personal and political. It isn't just that he is a liberal. Of course I disagreed with him violently on taxes, abortion, defense spending, welfare, and a host of policy issues. I have disagreed with many politicians in my life though, and never have my feelings been this intense. What sent me over the top about Clinton is that his brand of liberalism had an almost anti-American feel to it. Because it

received scant treatment in the press many Americans don't know that when the Clintons first moved into the White House, they seriously considered banning all military uniforms from White House grounds. From the generals briefing the president to the Marines guarding the front door, no one would have been allowed to wear a military uniform. Fortunately someone talked the Clintons out of this treachery, but take a moment to think about what even considering such a thing says about them. This was the president of the United States and his wife saying that something about military uniforms offended them. Apparently the noble symbols of martial honor and sacrifice so disturbed their unpatriotic, liberal sensibilities that they wanted to forbid them in the home of the nation's commander in chief. We should have kicked them out of office right then and there!

Yet it wasn't just Clinton's left-wing politics that incensed me. It was his character. In Washington we get a view of a man from the behind the scenes that the public rarely has a chance to see. The district really functions like a small town at times, something like the Mayberry of American politics. Staff members from different branches jog together; secretaries of different leaders meet for lunch, and conversations take place that no one expects will ever be repeated. But they are, and we often hear about a man's character long before his flaws become public. Even aside from this chattering, we learned quickly that the Clinton crowd had little respect for the institutions of our society. There was disrespect for the military. There were tales of disrespect for the Secret Service. There was disrespect for those serving in Congress. There was also the now infamous disrespect for the executive offices of the president, and of the White House itself. All of this, I believe, reflected on the Clinton character and the Clinton presidency. Remember when Clinton's people did thousands of dollars of damage to some of the White House offices just before the Bush administration took over in

2000? The Clintonites had conducted themselves that way for eight years because they were simply reflecting the nature of their boss.

The truth is that Bill Clinton was slimy. He came to office amid swirling accusations and rumors regarding his sexual misconduct, and of a kind that were astonishing even for Washington. Once he took office he quickly gained a reputation for dishonesty. Newt Gingrich once said in sincere surprise that "it was really hard to exaggerate how systematically, routinely dishonest Clinton was, and how really good he was at it." We heard this time and again, and from every level of government. People would walk out of a meeting with Clinton having shaken hands in agreement on something, and the next day Clinton or a staffer would call to say that he hadn't really meant what he had said. His reputation quickly soured everywhere he went. Rumors of his vile language, ill treatment of workers, and general slovenliness arose from the stewards on Air Force One, from the staff at Camp David, and from White House personnel.

I even gained an insight into his character through his golf game. I was watching television one day, and I saw Clinton playing golf with the first president Bush and late president Gerald Ford. Now Clinton had publicly claimed to have a 10 handicap, but I had a 10 handicap, and I could tell that Clinton was nowhere near it. I decided to ruffle his feathers a bit. I wrote him a letter telling him that I had watched his swing, that I knew he wasn't even close to a 10 handicap, and that I would play him anytime, anywhere, for any amount of money. He didn't write me back, but every time I was in an audience that he was addressing, he mentioned my note and how I had accused him of lying about his handicap. My challenge obviously bugged him, but he never had the guts to play me. The fact is that golf is a game of character, and you can tell who a man really is by how he plays. Clinton was as famous a cheater on the course as he was in life, and everyone close to him knew it.

Clinton's low character was revealed, as was the character of some Republican leaders, in the first major crisis of the postrevolution era— the 1995 government shutdown. As part of the Contract with America agenda Gingrich had been pushing for a balanced budget. He knew he didn't have the votes for a constitutional amendment that would mandate a balanced budget, but he was sure that he could accomplish his goal by 2002. The chairman of the House Budget Committee, John Kasich of Ohio, reported out a bill that trimmed $1 trillion, by spending cuts, and even eliminated executive departments like Education, Commerce, and Energy, along with nearly three hundred federal programs. This was just what we conservatives had come to Congress to do, and we were thrilled. The House passed this budget, 238 to 219, but the Senate failed as usual to agree on much of anything. Clinton urged his Democrats to slash away at the budget and enjoyed portraying the GOP as rigid, while he appeared open to compromise. He even had the temerity at one point to announce that "the era of big government is over." It may have been over, but this certainly wasn't any of his doing!

Meetings and negotiations took place all over Washington, and still a government shutdown loomed. It was during this time that some of my staff began to notice that Gingrich wasn't the tough guy he had presented himself to be. One of my senior staff members in those days, Tony Rudy, reported, "The Clinton White House figured out how to play Newt. They would put the *Time* magazine cover with Newt as the Man of the Year on the coffee table in front of where they would have Newt sit. Newt would come back into leadership meetings from the White House and tell us how the White House understood his significance. And people would look around and say to themselves, 'Have you lost your mind?'" I believe the Clinton people suspected they could manipulate Newt through appeal to his ego, because they were used to appealing to Clinton's ego. Apparently the tactic worked on Newt as well.

Negotiations spiraled downward, and after Clinton vetoed a stopgap spending bill, funding for government services ran out, and a shutdown began on November 13, 1995. Not long after, Gingrich made the mistake of his life. He told a room full of reporters that he forced the shutdown because Clinton had rudely made him and Bob Dole sit at the back of Air Force One and exit from the rear on a flight to the funeral of assassinated Israeli prime minister Yitzak Rabin. It was pitiful. The New York *Daily News* carried the headline "Cry Baby" above a drawing of Newt as a screaming baby in diapers. The Democrats even tried to take a blowup of the cover onto the floor of the House. Newt had been careless to say such a thing, and now the whole moral tone of the shutdown had been lost. What had been a noble battle for fiscal sanity began to look like the tirade of a spoiled child. On November 19, a truce was announced, and federal workers went back to work. For four weeks the House had tried to reach a budget deal but to no avail. On December 15, two weeks before Christmas, the government shut down again. This time the standoff lasted for twenty-one days.

I was concerned about the nearly quarter of a million government workers who were out of their jobs over the holidays, but I also knew that such expensive confrontations were the only way we were going to be able to change the course of liberal tax-and-spend economics. Big government had been feeding at the public trough too long, and we were in a position to put it on a diet—a drastic diet if necessary. I was willing to stay the course. I believed the long-term good outweighed any short-term pain. And I believed that Clinton was essentially spineless and would capitulate under political pressure if we just stuck to our guns. I was shocked then with what I heard from my television one Sunday evening in January as I was grilling steaks for some members at my condo. The news reported that Bob Dole was saying, "Enough is enough." The senior Republican in the Senate had caved in. Gingrich soon followed him.

I was ashamed of them. We lost the moral high ground, lost the battle of courage, and even lost out to Clinton's public relations game. The press portrayed the whole matter as a battle between a good and wise president on the one hand and a bunch of children having a temper tantrum on the other hand. The revolution, I can tell you, was never the same.

My friends and staff have often tried to talk me off the ledge on this issue, and they may be right. They contend that the shutdown actually did show courage and did convince Clinton to negotiate in better faith in the future. If this is true, the welfare reform bill that Clinton signed into law on August 22, 1996, was certainly an example of the change. We had made welfare reform a plank in the Contract with America, and we took it seriously. We knew the system wasn't working, and was outrageously expensive. Since 1965 the total cost of welfare had been $5.4 trillion. A number so big is hard to put into perspective. This meant that for each dollar spent on national defense in those years, $1.17 was spent on welfare. For every dollar spent on education at the local, state, and federal levels *combined*, 91 cents was spent on welfare. This was both tragic and, in my opinion, immoral.

More important than the cost was what was happening to people. Thousands of Americans simply got on welfare and never got off. Able-bodied people were morally and spiritually crippled by having government take care of them as though they were helpless. It was widely known that if a man had been on welfare all of his life until the age of twenty-one he was virtually unemployable. The system was destroying character, creating a permanent underclass, and preparing to pass the skyrocketing costs to the next generation.

We wanted to apply conservative principles to the welfare system. We believed that people needed to work and be responsible for themselves. Welfare needed to be limited support that didn't undermine families or character. So we proposed that the government stop making it profitable for women to have babies out of wedlock, stop breaking up families, stop rewarding teen pregnancies, stop giving welfare benefits to illegal immigrants, and set a two-year limit on welfare benefits so that people had to eventually find a job. In addition, we wanted to set a cap on welfare spending overall.

The negotiations over the welfare bill were tortuous and ego-driven, of course, but once the bill passed the results were astonishing. Welfare caseloads dropped from 8.4 million in 1996 to just over 3 million two years later, a 64 percent decrease. The average monthly number of welfare families fell in every state within those same two years. Welfare rolls decreased 22 percent. Nearly a year after the bill was signed 13 percent of adults formerly on welfare were working. A year after that 23 percent were working, and the trend has continued ever since.

These are just cold numbers, but consider what these numbers mean in human terms. Thousands of people who were once on welfare are now earning their way through life with their own hands. They are gaining skills, respect, and a sense of honor that welfare takes away. They are passing an ethic on to the next generation that will see their grandchildren living lives they could barely have dreamed of when they were on welfare. Perhaps most important of all, they are no longer slaves of the state. I am reminded of what Goldwater said: "I do not undertake to promote welfare, for I propose to extend freedom." This is what we did through the welfare bill, and what we would do on many other issues. We were in the business of extending freedom, and I was proud to play a role.

I wish I could say that I was as proud of our leadership as I was of our legislative successes. I wasn't. The fact is that we were not a cohesive team, and this hindered our ability to change the nation as we might have. Frankly, the majority of the blame for this has to be placed at Newt Gingrich's door.

Newt is an amazingly gifted man. He is intelligent, articulate, informed, and passionate to a fault. He was a wonderful field general who loved to fight and knew how to rally troops to battle. I still believe he was the right man for the job of creating a Republican revolution, and that the nation owes him a debt of gratitude. It is equally true, though, that he was an ineffective speaker of the House. He knew nothing about running meetings and nothing about driving an agenda. Most of us understood that it takes about two years to drive an agenda, and even then only with wise strategies and clockwork execution. Newt wanted to turn the ship of state on a dime. Nearly every other day he had a new agenda, a new direction he wanted us to take. It was impossible to follow him, and this was largely because he was beset with the classic academic's dysfunction: He thought that ideas alone were enough, that thinking made it so. If he had a new idea in his mind, he mistook its presence in his head for its presence in the real world. He had little understanding of how to make ideas into reality through a political system. I spent most of my time running around trying to develop an agenda that should have been his to create and drive.

Then there was Dick Armey, a gifted man, but a man so blinded by ambition as to be useless to the cause. Dick was a poor leader who also was contaminated by the academician's dysfunction, and was largely staff-driven. There were few fresh ideas coming from his direction. He was proud of being a nonconformist, Lone Ranger type, and even though Newt told him he would learn to "fly in formation," he never did. He resented me for being the other Texan on the leadership team, and he resented anyone he thought might get in the way of his becoming speaker of the House. Beware the man drunk with ambition. I think the rest of us were eager to drive a conservative agenda. Dick was eager to get to the top, and this lesser motivation made him a lesser figure on our team.

Making matters worse was the horrible environment that surrounded the leadership. There was backbiting and arguing, constant leaks and unending gossip. People became afraid to say anything, because ten minutes later it was leaked to the press. In time we learned where most of the leaks came from. There was a man on one of our staffs who had taken to leaking almost everything we said to reporters simply to win favor in support of his own ambitions. This self-serving fool helped create a culture of suspicion in which almost nothing of value could happen. What we did accomplish is even more amazing because of the environment in which we had to work.

During the four years in which Newt was the speaker we would meet with him from time to time to tell him that things had to change. He would agree, and we would try to develop strategies and tactics that would move us ahead in a consistent manner rather than in one that was changing nearly every day, as we had been. Before long, though, despite Newt's best intentions, we would be back in the swirling world of conflicting agendas and ideas, divorced from any meaningful process. It was frustrating to all of us and, in time, some members came to the end of their patience.

I soon learned that a group of congressmen were meeting secretly on their own to discuss how to make a change. The leaders of this group were Steve Largent, J. C. Watts, and Lindsey Graham. I knew that if dissatisfaction had risen to the level where members were meeting in secret to map out strategies of change, something truly had to be done soon. It was then that I made a mistake.

I decided to pull together a meeting of Paxon, Armey, and John Boehner, who was the chairman of the Republican conference, to try to handle the situation. Only too late would I realize that our meeting might look like part of a plot. It wasn't, but I wish now I had simply gone straight to Newt. We weren't conspiring in any way. We were trying to handle the crisis effectively. I certainly understand, though, how the meeting looks in retrospect to our critics.

In the days that followed rumors of a rebellion and the spirit of disgruntlement filled congressional offices. In time I agreed to meet with that growing group of furious congressmen who were led by Largent, Watts, and Graham. When I arrived at midnight for the meeting there were more than twenty-five congressmen eating pizza and discussing their concerns. I took a seat, and they immediately let me know that they intended to move to vacate the chair. This meant that they intended to call for a vote of no confidence in the speaker of the House. I tried to talk them out of it. I told them that they had the right to do it, though, but that they would need to think seriously about who they would support for speaker if they removed Gingrich. Would it be Armey? They said no. Few respected Armey, and even fewer thought he had the relationships with members to get anything done. Others said they didn't trust him. Perhaps Paxon would be their choice. They weren't sure, but they were ready to move.

Armey and Paxon were in Paxon's office waiting for my meeting to end, and when I returned I filled them in. I felt it was important for Armey to understand that he was not going to be speaker if this uprising succeeded. I still think this was the right thing to do, but apparently Armey went straight to Newt and told him that we had been plotting against him. This, of course, was a lie.

Not long after, I got word that Gingrich and Armey were in the speaker's office plotting a counterassault against us. Clearly Newt was under siege, but because of Armey's deception he had the wrong enemy in his sights. I decided to set him straight. I found Paxon and Hastert and went up to the speaker's office. Gingrich and Armey were just walking out of the door. Realizing that there was about to be a heated confrontation, Gingrich quickly pulled us all into his chief of staff's office. Instantly the shouting began. We told Newt we hadn't plotted against him, and that we had only tried to clean up the mess. We also let Armey know that we didn't appreciate his lie. In a truly moving moment Paxon turned to Newt and said, "Newt, if you believe this lie, I'll resign." Newt coolly accepted Paxon's resignation and tempers continued to rise. News reports of the confrontation—undoubtedly leaked by Armey— reported that I grabbed Armey's tie and threatened him. I didn't, but I sure wanted to.

When the confrontation ended, nothing had been resolved. I soon learned that Newt intended to embarrass Paxon, Hastert, and me by calling us before the entire Republican conference to account for ourselves. I was disappointed by this tactic, but I wasn't afraid. Ed Buckham, who was then my chief of staff, joined me in praying about the whole matter, and as I asked the Lord how I should approach the meeting, I sensed him saying, "Tell the truth." I remember laughing because it was so obvious. I hadn't planned *not* to tell the truth, but I had become so used to strategically planning my approach to every meeting that simply telling the truth sounded almost too good to be true. I did just that, though. I wrote down everything I had to say, and I even told the conference that I would largely read my comments so I didn't forget anything. I was as clear as I knew how to be. Yes, I had said I would vote to vacate the speaker's chair. Yes, I understood the frustration that many members felt. No, I had not participated in a plot; I had only worked to handle the situation constructively. And yes, I understood that Newt was wounded, dying the death of a thousand cuts, in Shakespeare's phrase. When I was done the conference gave me a standing ovation.

The field was now strewn with wreckage. In time Newt would decide not to run again for speaker, and would resign his seat. We eventually would be forced to choose his replacement just as one of the worst crises in American political history was unfolding. It goes without saying that my relationship with him had been destroyed. We had never been close, but we had managed a workable friendship both before and after I backed Madigan for minority whip, a friendship I had hoped to continue despite the storm of discontent over his poor leadership. Armey's lie had ended that possibility. I was livid. He had lied to cover his ambitions, betraying both his movement and his fellow leaders.

Among the saddest results of this affair was the loss of Bill Paxon. Over the years Bill had become one of my best friends. We shared both a passion for politics and for the smarter, more talented women we had married. Even apart from our friendship, though, Bill was the smartest politician I have ever known. He understood campaigns, the political process, and what gets people elected better than anyone. He had a feel for the things that motivate people politically and a sixth sense for human weakness. Perhaps more important, he knew what it takes to serve honorably and to serve well. I liked him, yes, but I admired him even more. If Newt was the general of the Republican revolution, Bill was the colonel. As the chair of the National Republican Campaign Committee he had kept us focused and moving in the right direction. He always had made sure we understood the unintended political consequences of everything we attempted. This had been invaluable, and had kept us from many destructive mistakes.

Sadly, Bill became Newt's scapegoat, though he had done nothing but try to help. Rumors circulated that not only had Paxon engineered the revolt against Newt but that he had resigned because he was gay and about to be "outted." This silly attempt at slander survived despite the fact that Bill was married to New York congresswoman Susan Molinari, and they had two beautiful daughters. Deeply wounded by the lies and suspicions around him, Bill resigned from Congress. The party and the nation are both poorer for it.

The period that ensued was one of Republican malaise. In the 1996 presidential election, Clinton defeated Bob Dole with 49 percent of the vote to Dole's 41 percent, largely because Ross Perot claimed the remaining 8 percent. Though Gingrich had bragged that Republicans would win 20 additional votes in the House, we ended up losing 3. In the midterm election of 1998 we lost 5 more. Sniffing party decline, some members began to grumble. One congressman even declared publicly, "The problem for the party is that Newt is the face of the party." If Republicans were not yet eating their young, they were at least beginning to nibble on each other.

The Democrats began to smell blood. In 1996 ethics charges were lodged against me, but of course they were dismissed. The same thing happened again, in 1998. At the time these seemed like minor occurrences, given the critical events happening around me. The truth is that both these ethics charges and those to come, as well as a lawsuit I would face in 1998, were all part of a carefully executed strategy by the Democrats. Rhode Island congressman Patrick Kennedy was the head of the Democratic Congressional Campaign Committee (DCCC) at the time, and he had announced on the DCCC's Web site his intention to go after me. Though I did not see it clearly, the Democrats intended to win by lawsuits and slander what they could not win at the ballot box or in Congress. James Carville groused to *Salon* magazine in 2002, "If Tom DeLay was a Democrat, we would control the House." Clearly the liberals wanted me gone.

So 1996 began ten years of political persecution, which I have to say Christine saw coming. She told me at the time that I had better get ready to fight back, because the Democrats were coming for me. I didn't believe her. I didn't think anyone in Congress could be that low. I also thought I had plenty of friends who would stand with me if a battle began. I was wrong on both counts, and as I'll explain more fully in a later chapter, these new tactics of the left have not only meant suffering for me and my family, but they will mean tragedy for the nation if they are allowed to continue. I'll say it again: Christine was right, I was wrong, and I will always regret ignoring her wise counsel.

It was during this time that a horrible tragedy occurred in the Capitol, one that brought fear and then grief to my professional family. On a quiet Friday afternoon in July 1998, I was sitting in my office in the Capitol building when I heard a sound like a china cabinet falling over. I did not know at first that the sound was actually gunfire. It turned out that a man had entered the Capitol through the Document Room door on the ground floor, and had walked around the metal detector. Without warning the man raised his .38 caliber pistol and shot the nearby guard, Officer Jacob J. Chestnut, in the head. A second officer, who was working a visitor's wheelchair through the door, saw what was happening and began firing at the shooter, who then dashed up some stairs, rounded a corner, and followed a woman toward my office complex. By this time I could tell shots had been fired, and I came out of my office to see what was going on. One of the men on my staff told me to get back into my office, and I could tell by his manner that we were all in danger.

A few moments later the shooter came through the outer doors of my office complex. A plainclothes policeman named John Gibson, who had long provided security for me, pulled his gun and confronted the shooter as he entered. The two shot each other at point-blank range. Immediately after, Capitol police arrived and took the wounded gunman into custody. The heroic Officer Gibson, who had saved all our lives, was rushed to the hospital.

Within moments of the incident the sergeant at arms, Bill Livingood, approached me and said, "I want you out of here. Since the shooter went directly to your office, we don't know whether this is a coordinated attempt on your life or not. Please leave." Bill knew I had a ticket for my usual flight back to Texas, and virtually ordered me to be on that plane. I did as he asked. I would later be criticized for leaving Washington during a crisis, but I was only doing what the senior law enforcement officer in the Capitol had instructed me to do. During that flight home I called back to my office to inquire about John Gibson. My staff told me that he had died on the way to the hospital. I began to sob, and I'm sure the whole plane heard me. It turned out that sitting on that same flight was Gene Green, a Democratic congressman from Texas, and when he saw my grief he arranged to sit with me so he could offer comfort. I have always been grateful for his kindness at that horrible moment. Later that evening, when we got word that this tragic event was the work of one lone gunman and not a broader conspiracy, Christine and I returned to Washington immediately.

The loss of John Gibson was a gut-wrenching tragedy. I had grown deeply fond of him. He was devoted to his job, and his love for his profession permeated everything he did. He took great care of my family, and it had been particularly endearing to see how he kept an eye on Dani. We had become friends, and often found time to talk about matters beyond work. I had a sign on my desk in those days that read "This Could Be the Day." I had heard the words in a Sunday school lesson, and they had challenged me. They could mean either that Jesus might return today or that I might die today. Either way they meant that I should be prepared spiritually, and should live out my purpose in life fully. John and I had often discussed the meaning of the words. He was Roman Catholic and approached his life on earth with a deep spirituality. Our discussions filled my mind as this valiant man lay in honor with his fellow officer four days after the shooting.

It turned out that the shooter was a forty-two-year-old lone gunman named Russell Eugene Weston, Jr., from Rimini, Montana. Psychiatric tests confirmed that he was a paranoid schizophrenic. He has still not been tried for the two murders, the courts having found that he isn't mentally competent. The shooting could have taken far more lives than it did, though, and while I was grateful, I suppose that my feelings were the same as Trent Lott's, who said at the Capitol memorial service, "It was a death in the family."

The grief I felt over John's murder that summer would merge with feelings about the historic congressional crisis of that fall to make 1998 one of the most difficult years of my life. Washington had long been filled with rumors both of Bill Clinton's infidelities, and of possible illegalities surrounding the Whitewater land transactions; in time, the accusations regarding the latter of these grew so severe that a three-judge panel had appointed a special prosecutor named Kenneth Starr to investigate. It was not long before Starr's authority was broadened from the Whitewater investigation to include investigation of possible perjury and obstruction of justice by Clinton to cover up his affair with a White House intern, Monica Lewinsky, in the Oval Office. These new charges arose because, in sworn testimony before a grand jury in January 1998, Clinton had denied that he had had any improper relations with Lewinsky, as he would continue to before his family, staff, and friends.

Though I certainly understood a man's sexual temptations, I was disgusted by the sordid details that filled news reports each day, just like most Americans were. Still, I wasn't surprised that Clinton would behave in such a manner, and I knew that adultery, even in the Oval Office, wasn't a crime. I just hoped the whole thing would go away. Besides, the American people had elected this immoral character twice, and I assumed we would have to live with him until the end of his allotted eight years. Then, in a televised appearance on August 17, Clinton admitted that he had carried on an "inappropriate" affair with Lewinsky. This meant that the president of the United States had lied under oath before a grand jury. Immediately I realized that the issue wasn't sex, it was the rule of law. Could the nation's highest law enforcement official be allowed to continue in office after breaking the law himself?

Unfortunately, this wasn't the issue that most Americans were thinking about. During the summer of that year Newt Gingrich had made the decision, along with Minority Leader Dick Gephardt, to take all of the grand jury transcripts and put them on the Internet. Now, rather than focusing on the crime committed by the president, the nation was swirling with reports of semen-stained dresses and cigars used as sex toys. The late-night talk show hosts had plenty of juicy tidbits for their monologues, and more than one father felt the humiliation of having to explain the cigar and the dress to his children. Everyone's focus was on the sex, but the sex was not the primary legal issue.

Even before Clinton's perjury came to light I believed his conduct was so beneath his office that he should resign, and I decided to issue a call for just that. I discussed my decision with Newt first, who chewed me out for even considering such a move. I listened carefully to all of his reasons, but I thought they amounted to nothing more than politics, and I believed that there were greater matters to consider. I then scheduled a conference call with the leadership. As each man expressed his agreement with calling on Clinton to resign, Newt saw the wisdom of our plan and got onboard. The decision made, I knew I could call for the president's resignation with a clear conscience and the backing of our leadership. This was all before we learned that the president had broken the law.

When Congress returned to business in September Kenneth Starr's office delivered thirty-six boxes of documents to the House with an investigator's report concluding that Clinton's actions "may constitute grounds for impeachment." On October 8, the House passed a resolution, 258 to 176, instructing the Judiciary Committee, chaired by Henry Hyde of Illinois, to examine the evidence to determine whether the

NO RETREAT, NO SURRENDER

president had committed impeachable offenses or "whether it was just something personal and not a matter of national concern." Two months later Hyde's committee concluded that the president had "committed perjury and obstructed justice." Furthermore, they agreed that "it would be a dereliction of duty if we didn't proceed . . . with impeachment with a view towards removing him from office."

I agreed with the Judiciary Committee completely, and decided to work for Clinton's impeachment. I have taken a lot of heat for this decision in the years since, but I have absolutely no regrets in the matter. The fact is that there were military personnel in jail at the time for the same lie under oath that Clinton had committed, and he was their commander in chief. The rule of law had to prevail if the rule of law was to continue to mean anything in our country. I believed then and I believe now that Bill Clinton had to be impeached, and it was the responsibility of Congress to do it. This is the whole reason for the separation of powers—to hold each branch of government accountable to the law and to the people. The executive branch clearly could not govern itself in this matter, and so it would fall to Congress to hold the president responsible for his criminal act. It wasn't about politics. It wasn't about sex. It was about a perjury and the rule of law.

Unfortunately, our leadership was in no moral shape to press the case. I have learned in my years that a guilty conscience robs a man of moral resolve. At the very moment in our history when the president of the country was violating both his marriage vows and the law, the congressional leaders who should have held the moral line were too compromised by their own misdeeds to act righteously. It is now public knowledge that Newt Gingrich was having an affair with a staffer during the entire impeachment crisis. Clearly, men with such secrets are not likely to sound a high moral tone at a moment of national crisis. And there would be more Republicans exposed.

Nevertheless, using the methods we had perfected over the years in our "grow the votes" efforts, my team worked the vote for impeachment. It certainly wasn't a normal whip operation. I believed that many members who were hesitant would make the right choice if only they were given the facts. We decided to put the most telling documents in a secure room and encouraged the members to spend time there learning the details of the testimony against Clinton. It was stunning to read of the affairs, the allegations of rape, and the lies used as a cover-up. I knew most of the members were people of integrity and would accept the truth if given an opportunity.

Some Republicans and nearly all Democrats wanted Congress to censure the president rather than impeach him. I believed that censure wasn't enough, that the president had to be punished, and that impeachment was the proper punishment. I expected that he wouldn't be driven from office because the votes weren't there for it in the Senate. Still, I believed the right thing had to be done.

As ready for battle as I was, I was not prepared for the dramatic events that would unfold in late December. Weeks before, when Bob Livingston had announced his candidacy to replace Newt as speaker, I had been disappointed, but I had committed to working with him. I didn't think Bob was speaker material, but my job was to make him a success, not to whine that he wasn't my first choice. Not long after he announced, though, a reporter dug up information about an affair. Bob went before the Republican conference, told them that he had indeed had an affair but that it was long over, and that he was truly sorry that the conference had to be bothered with it. Most members were satisfied, but some had their doubts that Bob was the best candidate for speaker.

Concerns about his previous affair continued to mount, and a growing number of congressmen began questioning whether he was the right man for speaker, given our efforts to impeach Clinton. Even while Bob

was hiring staff and setting up in the speaker's office, the grumbling and uncertainty continued. I finally went to him the night before the impeachment vote and told him that things were getting bad, and that we had seven days to save his speakership. I noticed that he turned completely white as I laid out the strategy he had to follow if he was going to survive. The next morning, while I was working out at the gym, I got a call from Bob. He asked me to come to his office immediately. When I arrived I could feel the tension. We were all wound tighter than a drum, but no one was tighter than Bob when I walked into that room. He told me that he had decided not to stand for speaker, that the pressure on him in light of the allegations against Clinton was too great, and that he knew he was done.

I confess that I broke down and cried. I grieved not only for Bob but for what this meant for the party and for the country. Within a matter of a week we were supposed to start a speaker's race, impeach a president, and open a new session of Congress. It was almost too much, and I was undone. I left Bob and went to find Denny Hastert, my friend and ally. When I told him what was about to happen he, too, was shaken. Then I told him what I knew would shock him even more: "Denny, you've got to be speaker." He turned white and protested, "No, no, no." The choice was obvious, though.

I had considered running for the speakership myself some time before, but after three weeks of intense prayer I knew I wasn't the right man for the job. Besides, I had become "nuclear" politically due to my role in impeaching Clinton. No, I certainly could not be speaker, and this made the decision an easy one. Newt was gone. Armey could never get the votes. Paxon was leaving. Livingston was compromised. Hastert was the only man who could do the job.

He was not convinced, though. I called Bill Paxon, and the two of us beat up on Denny for several hours. Denny is a good man, and he would

never presume to take such a huge responsibility upon himself without serious deliberation. He thought, argued, thought some more, and then began to acquiesce. As he did I asked him the question that had to be asked: "Denny, are there any skeletons in your closet? Tell me now if there are. Is there anything I need to know?" He assured me that there was nothing, and I was relieved. A few moments later Denny asked me to leave him alone. I learned later that he spent the next forty minutes on his knees, praying. While he did that Newt called me on my cell phone. He said that he'd heard about Livingston, and that Hastert had to be the speaker. I told him what had been happening, and what was probably happening right then behind Denny's door. This set Newt at peace.

When Denny emerged from his office he said simply, "Okay, I'll do it." Immediately I knew what I had to do next: leave town. I know it may sound as though I abandoned my friend at a critical moment. It had to happen, though. It was absolutely vital that Hastert not be seen as DeLay's boy. He had to stand on his own, ascend to the speakership as a matter of his own choice, and win the vote as a result of his own efforts. I did not whip the vote for him, and I did not pull any strings. Denny Hastert became speaker of the House because he thought he was the right man for the role, and because enough members agreed with him.

All of this, of course, was unfolding in the background of what Americans were seeing on their television sets. On December 19, Livingston went on the floor of the House and made the speech of his life. After talking about his love of Congress and respect for each member, he addressed Clinton: "To the president, I would say, sir, you have done great damage to this nation" but "you have the power to terminate that damage and heal the wounds that you have created. You, sir, may resign your post." The Democrats immediately began shouting, "No, no, no." Then they changed to, "You resign. You resign." Livingston raised his hand for silence, and then said, "I can only challenge you in such fash-

ion if I am willing to heed my own words. So I must set the example that I hope President Clinton will follow. I will not stand for speaker of the House. I shall vacate my seat in approximately six months into the 106th Congress." The room went silent, and moments later it burst into applause as Livingston left the chamber. That same day the House impeached Clinton on two of the five charges against him.

On January 5, 1999, Denny was nominated unanimously by the Republican conference and elected by the House the following day. Then, on February 9, after nearly five weeks of testimony and deliberation, the Senate voted against his removal, and acquitted the president. I was not surprised by this, bold action being nearly impossible for the Senate, but I finished this dramatic episode proud of the House of Representatives and its heroic stand for the rule of law.

It would be hard to exaggerate the transformation that occurred under Denny Hastert. Our leadership became cohesive. In an environment of trust and clear communication, we became extremely effective. We knew our jobs, and we carried them out. We worked on a defined agenda, and we stayed with it until we were successful. The eight years of Denny Hastert's speakership were without question the most enjoyable and rewarding years of my political career.

The Hastert years would bridge the terms of two presidents, Clinton and Bush. In the vacuum created by Clinton's moral swirl and poor leadership we were able to make huge strides for conservative principles. We had projected that we would balance the budget within seven years, and we ended up doing it in two. We used the nearly $550 billion that we saved to pay down debt rather than allow Clinton to spend it on liberal fantasies. We resisted Clinton's attempt to make even deeper cuts in military spending than he did, and thank God for it, given the defense needs of post-9/11 America.

In the Bush years we passed one of the most historic bills of my time in Congress—the Medicare reform bill. When we came to power Medicare was broke, and it was so expensive it was in danger of carrying the economy of the country down with it. It was also a symbol of government stupidity. Newspapers widely reported the fact that on the Medicare plan the government would pay forty thousand dollars for a diabetic to have his feet surgically removed because of the ravages of his disease, but that Medicare would not pay one hundred dollars a month for Glucophage, a drug that could save a diabetic's feet. Medicare also denied drugs seniors desperately needed, but instead paid huge bills for lengthy hospital stays that were necessary only because the right drugs weren't available in the first place. Such follies riddle the program.

Again, we applied conservative principles. We injected an element of choice. We instituted systems of competition that kept prices down and quality up. We involved the private sector. We instituted health savings accounts, which allowed people to take responsibility for their own health care. We even improved the prescription drug program. Not too surprisingly, in less than a year Medicare began saving money, the cost of prescriptions began to drop, and the program ceased being a drain on the country's economy. Of course, the press caught virtually none of this, because old hippy, liberal editors were too busy bitching that we had dared to tinker with one of their cherished social programs. The fact is that we used conservative principles to make failing social programs serve the people better, and it is the people these liberals are supposed to be caring about, isn't it? Perhaps the truth is that they only care about increasing the power of the state. Whatever the case, we made government better by shrinking it, involving the free market, and giving people choice. It works every time.

The other huge legislative success of the Bush years was the No Child Left Behind legislation, and here I found myself in conflict with the president. I do not believe that the federal government ought to be involved in the educational system. I believe education ought to be a matter for state and local governments, which are better able to tailor their schools for their unique region and populace. The president's support for No Child Left Behind forced me to make a decision: Should I make life hell for him on his pet legislation, or should I support him? It was not an easy choice, but I decided that it wasn't my duty to take one of the main promises of the president's campaign for office and try to defeat him on it. I worked with the administration, got the legislation to the floor, and then voted against it. It was passed nevertheless, and accomplished exactly what the president intended. George W. Bush has spent three times what Clinton did on public education.

In the Bush years the nation would endure the horrors of September 11, 2001, the resulting wars, Hurricane Katrina, and a rising tide of illegal immigration. These were defining events that would leave a lasting imprint on the political direction of the country. Unfortunately, while these historic crises unfolded, I was forced to deal with an increasingly vicious assault from the political left in this country, one that would ultimately convince me that I would be better able to help shape events from outside the Congress than from within. This assault was launched by the liberals in Congress who, knowing that they could not win the battle of ideas, chose to lead a coalition devoted to the politics of personal destruction and to the criminalization of political disagreement. In the early days I ignored their lies and rage as the typical tantrums of an angry minority. Eventually, though, I realized that the left fully intended to destroy me with the most vicious and immoral tactics imaginable. This will sound to some like paranoia. It is not. It is the truth of my experience and the truth about a dangerous trend in American politics. To warn of this trend and fully explain my fight to the nation, I must do in this book what I was forced to do in life: turn from the battle for conservative values to the battle against liberal lies.

TEN LIBERAL LIES YOU'VE
HEARD ABOUT ME

It was Winston Churchill who once said, "In war a man dies only once, but in politics many times." No one who enters public office is surprised by this anymore. Political leadership has always been tantamount to painting a target on your back, and this is even more the case in our media-driven, "inside story"–addicted generation. Only a fool would step on the public stage today without expecting every detail of his life to be exposed, debated, and criticized. This is simply the price of leadership in our time.

There is something else happening today, though, that must come to an end if this country is going to have serious leaders at its helm. Today it is not enough to defeat a man politically. It is not even enough to vilify him publicly. You have to carpet bomb his life. You have to make sure that he leaves office disgraced, bankrupt, and heading for jail. You have to ruin him in every way, and then dance on his grave. This is what the political left in this country has brought us, and this is why many of the best leaders in our land refuse to take public office. They are willing to be scarred in political battle, but they are not willing to subject themselves to total destruction.

I remember when Ray Donovan, Ronald Reagan's secretary of labor, was acquitted of corruption charges in a court of law after a prolonged trial by media. Stepping to the microphone on the day of his victory, he said, "Where do I go to get my reputation back?" These were tragic words that warned of what a man might suffer for serving his country. Today, though, a man should count himself fortunate if all he loses is his reputation. He could easily lose everything he owns, the legacy he intended to leave to his children. He could lose his right to work in his chosen profession, and might very likely end up serving time in jail. This is what the criminalization of politics and the politics of personal destruction have left us.

I served in the United States Congress for twenty-two years. I was passionate, aggressive, and partisan. I believed in my cause, and I hit hard. It came as no surprise to me then when my political opponents hit back. To open my morning paper and see lies written about me, or to see myself painted in the ugliest terms, became a regular part of my life. It was harder to read vicious distortions about my family and friends, but even this I accepted as the price we all paid for the life of leadership I had chosen to pursue.

What I did not expect was a concerted effort to destroy me legally, financially, and personally. I have now spent millions of dollars in lawyers' fees to answer the lies of the left. I have taken hours away from doing the nation's business to work through the laborious process of responding to legal charges that my liberal opponents knew were untrue and frivolous when they first filed them. I have watched my family suffer under the burden of not just my political misfortunes—an expected reality in a politician's family—but of the threat of material destruction, imprisonment, and ruin. This should not be what happens to someone who has defended his political ideals, aggressively, yes, but honorably. A congressman serves his nation by serving his values with passion, and the nation only suffers when partisanship is punished with personal destruction.

I use this word "punished" because it is the best description of what is really happening. I did not serve in Congress for twenty-two years because I simply stumbled into the role or captured it in some illegal way. I was elected by people who thought I was the best representative of their values. Once elected I fought hard for conservative principles and, in time, my fellow conservatives and I won major victories. Remember, these were victories for the very principles we were sent to Congress to serve.

But the liberals could not win on the floor or at the ballot box, so they tried to win by hurting us personally. Like good communists, when they cannot defeat their enemies politically they seek to destroy them personally, and this is what they did to us. All of this is punishment for holding values different from theirs. All of this is the price they want to visit on us simply for being conservative.

I began paying this price shortly after the Republican revolution got under way, when it became clear to the Democrats that our success in 1994 with voters was no fluke. Democratic leadership became intent on driving me from politics. For the next decade I would endure constant harassment in the press, ethics charges, lawsuits, and, in short, a concerted effort to destroy me politically and personally. All of this was part of a coordinated effort led by Patrick Kennedy, then head of the Democratic Congressional Campaign Committee (DCCC), who had determined that since he could not defeat me on the issues, he would try to defeat me with lawsuits and ethics charges. This is why, following two earlier sets of ethics charges, Kennedy filed a RICO suit against me.

Now RICO—Racketeering-Influenced Corrupt Organization—laws are about preventing criminal conspiracies. Kennedy's DCCC sued me for conspiring to defeat Democrats. This sounds like a horrible joke, but it wasn't. Being found guilty of a RICO suit can mean huge fines, and even jail time. I ended up spending over five hundred thousand dollars defending myself before the case was finally dropped. It was, without question, one of the most vicious lawsuits in American history. Yet it achieved its purpose. It allowed Kennedy's allies in the liberal press to report that Tom DeLay was being charged with corruption. This was the intent all along: to smear me with false accusations before the watching public. And it was only the beginning of my troubles.

Within a few years Nancy Pelosi became the House minority leader, and she took the lead in the Democrats' smear campaign. Her arena of her dirty work was the House floor. It became routine for her to move a "privileged motion," which is a motion a minority leader is permitted to offer, and which allows her then to speak on her motion before the House and the media. What follows is usually a vote either to table the motion or to act on it. Pelosi knew that none of her motions would be acted upon by a Republican-dominated House, but all she really wanted was the chance to make speeches attacking me and other Republicans before the members and, of course, the press. Many was the time she would move a privileged motion and make a speech filled with wild accusations, and I would later find liberal newspapers reporting only that Tom DeLay's corruption had been the topic of House debate.

While Pelosi used her privileges as the House minority leader to smear me, other congressmen used their special order time to carry Pelosi's lies to the American people. Remember that this special order time was mandated by a House rule that let any member take the floor after the House had finished its business and speak for an hour on any subject he chose. This is the tactic that Newt Gingrich had used so effectively. The presence of the C-SPAN cameras even after the House had finished its business had allowed Newt to speak to the nation, and he wisely chose to teach the nation about the elements of a conservative worldview. In the case of the Democrats, men like Jim McDermott of Washington state used this special order time to attack me and other Republican leaders. This meant that before a national audience I was being held aloft as the author of the culture of corruption in the nation's capital.

What emerged was the perfect storm of personal destruction. Between Pelosi and her puppets doing their worst on the floor of Congress, the liberal press echoing their lies, and a host of supposedly independent organizations like CREW (Citizens for Responsibility and Ethics in Washington), Common Cause, and Democracy 21, among others, filing suits and pressing ethics charges, I soon found myself in a sea of litigation and public misrepresentation.

Now laying aside for a moment that these tactics were unethical, un-American, and, in some cases, immoral, the hypocrisy of the assault against me is that some who questioned my ethics have had their own questioned by Republicans. Rahm Emanuel, who followed Patrick Kennedy as head of the DCCC, not only made millions of dollars in an inexplicably short period of time, but is also accused of using public employees in his campaign. Nancy Pelosi took a trip to Puerto Rico that has come under suspicion because it was paid for by lobbyists. A federal court held that Jim McDermott was actually found guilty of a crime that violated a federal law by obstructing and giving the tape of an interpreted private conversation among members of the Republican leadership to the *New York Times*. The case is currently on appeal. Then there is William Jefferson, the congressman from Louisiana, who is being investigated for taking a bribe and was caught by the FBI with ninety thousand dollars in his freezer. Clearly the Democrats have some housecleaning to do, but they seem to prefer the tactics of personal destruction to living up to their own rhetoric about ethics.

The strength behind all of the efforts against me, of course, was the power of the big lie, and this is what brings us to the business of this chapter. I have thought long and hard about how to respond to the liberals' barrage. Of course I must answer in court, because this is required by our legal system. That is, if I ever get to court: Clearly my opponents want to file lawsuits against me for the sake of smearing my name, but they never seem to be willing to take those suits into court, where they will have to prove their facts. Beyond legalities, though, I have tried to decide between rising above my opponents and refusing to validate their charges by even mentioning them or answering them directly and shaming them with the truth. I've decided on the latter, but the reasons may come as a surprise. I am not doing this just to save my reputation. That will happen with time anyway, because the truth is on my side. Nor am I doing this because I have some driving need to answer each lie in detail.

No, I want to shame these lies with the truth because I believe this may help to expose the tactics that are keeping good people from public office and punishing those who serve well. I want to take the risk of repeating lies about me so I can demonstrate how these lies are designed to bludgeon me for simply having the wrong political views. Perhaps then I can help to end our current culture of political bloodletting before it permanently sullies our nation. We cannot continue to allow liberals to function like communists and destroy anyone who gets in their way. The only way I know to do this is by being direct, unsparing, and brutally honest as I answer the ten most often repeated liberal lies about Tom DeLay.

Lie Number 1: Tom DeLay took trips illegally paid for by corporations and lobbyists, which he rewarded with political favors.

It does not bother me that people think I'm corrupt; that can be disproven when I get to court. What bothers me is that people think I'm stupid. Would I, the most investigated man in America, really be so fool-ish as to take an illegal, high-profile trip and give my enemies a weapon to hurt me with? No, I would not, nor have I ever accepted any illegal travel.

Let's start at the beginning, though. I believe in the private sector. I love the free market, and I think that business is not an evil in our na-tion but one of the great engines of betterment for human beings. On the other hand, I believe that government ought to be small, and as light a burden as possible on the backs of the people. Therefore, when I travel, as a congressman must, I would prefer that private money fund the trip if possible, rather than the taxpayers.

Many politicians feel differently. They love traveling on the public dime and take CODEL—short for "congressional delegation"—trips by the dozens. I disagree. I would rather a private foundation fund my travel if at all possible, and so I've taken very few CODELs in my twenty-two years in Congress. In fact, I haven't traveled very much at all. In one ten-year period while I was in Congress I only traveled out of the country twice.

The press and their liberal lords have worked hard to paint my travel as some sinister conspiracy. For them words like "corporate," "lobby-ist," and "private" are vile. For example, in 2000 I took a trip to Scot-land and England at the invitation of conservative politicians in those countries. They wanted to learn how we had won such a great victory in 1994, and how we had accomplished the Contract with America. It was a wonderful experience. We flew on a private plane and held miniseminars with our fellow conservatives overseas, and I had the privilege of meeting with Margaret Thatcher, one of my heroes. I also got to play a few rounds of golf, which I try to do as often as I can when I travel. On this trip I had the once-in-a-lifetime opportunity to play at St. Andrews, the legendary birthplace of golf and a mecca for all true players. The trip was paid for by the National Center for Public Policy Research and was completely aboveboard.

When I returned home you would have thought I had joined Al Qaeda. The press talked about the trip like it was part of a conspiracy to overthrow the government, and the House Ethics Committee was asked to investigate. Of course there was nothing unethical about it at all. I urged the Ethics Committee to address the charges, but they never did. Still, because Americans have been trained by the press to conclude that a congressman holding a cigar and a golf club while on a privately funded trip must be plotting evil, the aura of impropriety hovers over this trip and a number of others I have made.

And what about those political favors? Well, they didn't exist. But let me take this whole issue a bit further. A congressman only accepts trips to study an industry or a cause if he is already somewhat committed in the first place. If I'm interested in helping the nursing home industry or airplane manufacturers or construction workers, I'll travel to study their issues only because I already lean toward serving them in some way. So if I return to the floor of the House and vote for legislation that aids construction workers, this doesn't mean I've done anything illegal or in any way contrary to the best interests of the nation. In fact, I've served the country by giving an informed vote.

One more thing: Because liberals and the press are influenced by socialism's hatred of the private sector they speak of business people and corporations like they are the evil empire. Not only is this a silly lie that defies history and reason, the vital truth is that a congressman is sworn to represent the people in private industry just as surely as he is public school teachers and policemen. Not only should we be thankful for what the private sector has accomplished in this country, we should start recognizing that those who work in that sector have a right to political representation also. A close look at their spending on political

NO RETREAT, NO SURRENDER

lobbying will reveal that they actually spend less than labor unions do to achieve their political goals.

So yes, I took a trip to Scotland. Yes, I played golf. Yes, it was privately funded. And yes, it was both legal and informative. If I had the opportunity, I would do it again.

Lie Number 2: Tom DeLay introduced a culture of corruption into Washington through his K-Street Project.

Liberals blaming me for corruption in Washington is like the KKK blaming Martin Luther King, Jr., for an epidemic of burning crosses. Still, I understand why the K-Street Project so enrages the left: It is their own tactics turned against them.

When the revolution of 1994 made Republicans the majority in the House for the first time in forty years I hoped we could change three cultures in Washington: the political culture; the media culture; and the K Street, or lobbyist, culture. I think we accomplished the first of these. Largely due to Newt Gingrich's efforts in the House as a whole, and to my efforts within the party apparatus, we improved the way Congress and political parties function. We had almost no ability, and therefore almost no success, in changing the media culture. In fact, it may have worsened during our years in power. The K Street culture was a different story. I knew we could change this Democratic stronghold if we would just be firm. And we were.

Americans have not seemed very interested in that strip of lobbying firms gathered along K Street in their nation's capital. When HBO unveiled a hip miniseries called *K-Street* a few years ago the show died of neglect, and this lack of interest is just the reason the whole lobbying industry remains a mystery to most Americans. This is also why the press is able to raise such undue suspicions.

When we came to power in 1994 most lobbying firms were headed by Democrats, staffed by Democrats, and funded Democratic initiatives with millions of dollars. In fact, K Street had actually been built by the Democratic majority over the previous fifty years or so. Then they had to deal with us. Picture it: A senior lobbyist would sit in my office. He was a liberal heading a liberal firm, and he was putting thousands if not millions of dollars into liberal coffers. But he wanted access and cooperation from me, even though I was in office to execute a conservative agenda.

So we started playing hardball. First, I would ask if there were any Republicans in the firms of the lobbyists I met with and, if so, I would ask to meet with them in the next meeting rather than the liberals. Second, if there were no Republicans in the firm, or just a token few, I would suggest that if they wanted to deal with us they ought to start hiring people who spoke our language and held our values. I also had no problem telling lobbying firms that someone specific they intended to hire wasn't going to win them any favor with us. This, again, was simply an attempt to make them consider our values as they attempted to work with us.

Don't come into my office asking me to support legislation to help you, and then turn around and give tens of thousands of dollars to support a liberal agenda and liberal politicians who are seeking to undermine everything we are trying to do. This was political hardball, but it was only asking that we have what the Democrats had had when they were in the majority. Remember that you get to be the majority because a majority of the people elects you. So we were insisting that the lobbyists get behind the direction of the country rather than undermine it with their money while looking to us for cooperation.

Let's speak bluntly about this matter of money. The problem is not that there is too much money spent in politics. The problem is that there isn't enough money spent in politics. Americans spend more money on potato chips than they do on all political races put together, yet government determines just about everything in their lives. We need to grow up as a country and realize that politics is something worthy of investment, and that it isn't dirty to fund those who support your values as they contend in the political arena. The truth is that money is speech. People should be free to spend their money in support of their words and their values.

People often ask me how I am able to raise so much money. It is very simple: I believe in what I'm doing. I tell potential donors that people like me are working their butts off to advance conservative values, and that those outside the battlefield should give to make victory for our values possible. We are trying to do good here. It is hard and it is expensive. Give so that we can turn the country in the right direction. That's it. When you are that honest and that straightforward, people respond. I simply refuse to apologize for raising money in support of some of the most important principles in human history.

Having said this, though, I never raise money for myself. In fact, even my enemies concede that I live modestly and never feather my own nest. In one of the most vicious anti-DeLay books the authors said, "Critics looking for behavior that suggests DeLay has used his position in leadership to enrich himself have found nothing." This is the truth, and donors sense it. I'll raise millions for my cause if I can, but I'm not about making money for myself through political fund-raising. This would be a betrayal of my cause.

There is another charge that parallels the K-Street Project allegation, and this is that I involved lobbyists in drafting legislation. Yes I did, and would again. Remember that I am devoted to the power of the free market. With the start of the Republican revolution I was trying to deregulate everything I could to get government off the backs of the people, as Ronald Reagan said, and liberate the private sector to achieve its best. Should I have turned to the supposed "experts" sitting in the conference rooms of the regulatory agencies? No. Should I turn to "experts" in the universities? No. These people are part of the problem: liberals who think every need is best met with another dose of big government. I needed people to help me think through policy from a free market perspective, and minds like that were in the private sector. Yes I invited them to the deregulation party, because they knew more about the details than anyone else. My reasoning is simple: If you want to get government regulations off the backs of energy producers, for example, talk to the energy producers about how government gets in their way. Then get their government affairs people to help you draft legislation. You'll certainly get better results than you would by talking to the Environmental Protection Agency or the energy experts at Harvard.

The fact is that liberals are upset about the K-Street Project because it was our attempt to make the lobbying industry values-driven. We announced that business as usual was over and that ideology was our first consideration. There was nothing corrupt or underhanded about this. It was simply one of many approaches we took to champion the values the American people had elected us to represent.

Lie Number 3: Tom DeLay was repeatedly found guilty of ethics violations by the House Ethics Committee.

Unfortunately, ethics charges in the House of Representatives have become so politicized you can't trust what you hear about them anymore. But let me start with a clear statement of the truth. Was Tom DeLay ever found guilty of ethics violations by the House Ethics Committee? No. Not once. Not ever.

There have been ethics charges connected to my conduct filed before the Ethics Committee perhaps half a dozen times since I entered Congress. Each time they've been dismissed. In some cases the bipartisan committee chastised the person who made the charges for abusing the process.

Let me give you one example of this. In 2004 ethics charges were filed against me by a Democratic congressman from Texas named Chris Bell. In league with a far-left organization called CREW—Citizens for Responsibility and Ethics in Washington—Bell accused me of taking a bribe from Westar Energy Corporation in return for my support for specific legislation. The charges were false, of course, but that didn't stop Bell and his liberal henchmen. Now CREW's name sounds all noble and benevolent. Who can argue about responsibility and ethics? The fact is that CREW is a liberal organization that goes after the national leaders it does not like by using lawsuits and ethics charges, and this is why they joined Chris Bell in attacking me.

I should mention that Bell's charges broke a seven-year gentlemen's agreement between Democrats and Republicans that they would not use ethics charges as political weapons against each other. Clearly, Bell is no gentleman. Thankfully, the Ethics Committee not only responded to the charges with no sanctions against me, but they chastised him for, in their words, filing a complaint against me containing "innuendo, speculative assertions or conclusory statements" in violation of the committee rules. Still, this is how the noble processes of Congress are being subverted by the political left in this country.

It is true that the committee has upon occasion admonished me in response to ethics charges. An admonishment is not a sanction, though. It is a warning that a member of Congress should reexamine their conduct and consider making corrections. Usually this is done in private, and is a matter of honorable correction among members.

In recent years, though, even the process of a slight admonishment has been used as an opportunity to humiliate. In three of the times the Ethics Committee admonished me, they not only made the charges public but released the supporting documentation to the public. I wouldn't have minded if this had been their regular practice, but their actions were a break from precedent and purely for political reasons. They gave the press the chance to repackage the charges to make them look like something serious. They weren't, and that is why the committee dismissed them with only an admonishment.

I should say that each time I received an admonishment from the Ethics Committee, I completely rejected their warnings. I had done nothing wrong. The rules are clear, and I had stayed within them. I understood that the admonishments were more about publicly embarrassing me than they were about any serious ethical misconduct. I felt then as I do now that the Ethics Committee had become a tool of partisan politics rather than the unbiased, nonpartisan entity it was designed to be.

Surprisingly, most of these abuses of the Ethics Committee's prerogatives were the work of a Republican, Joel Hefley of Colorado. Hefley had been a mediocre member who wanted desperately to chair the Armed Services Committee. I thought he was not the right man for that job, and I worked with others to block this appointment. He is a notoriously angry man, though, and set himself up to oppose me. Not long afterward he became the chair of the Ethics Committee, and my life immediately became more difficult. Hefley thought nothing of violating precedents to embarrass me, though he should have known the charges against me were frivolous. Sadly, this is what politics has done to the righteous policing of ethics in the House of Representatives. It has become part of the larger Washington culture of destroying your enemies.

By the way, when Hefley was rotated off of the chairmanship of the Ethics Committee, the press alleged that Denny Hastert had removed the man to get him off my back. Nothing could have been further from the truth. The fact is that when the Republican revolution took place, one of the reforms we instituted was to limit committee chairmanships to three terms, or six years. Hefly's six years were up, and he would have left the committee no matter who was speaker. The odd thing is that the press is always complaining about the "old-boy network" in Congress. We Republicans finally get the chance to institute rules to break up that network, and the press complains when one of their favorites is removed from his chairmanship. This is the nature of blind partisanship in Washington and the environment that has politicized ethics allegations.

Lie Number 4: Tom DeLay blocked the progress of basic civil rights in the Mariana Islands.

It is odd to me that the harder I work to champion freedom, the more the left accuses me of supporting slavery. This must be what George Orwell meant by "doublespeak."

Except for their strategic importance during World War II, the Mariana Islands weren't important to anyone on the left until they became a shining example of what an unrestrained free market can do. The Navy governed the islands after the war until 1962, and then they were transferred to the Department of the Interior. This lasted until 1975, when the islanders voted for self-rule, though this promise was largely neglected until Ronald Reagan gave the people what they wanted—freedom to determine their own destiny.

Prior to self-rule the islands had been a welfare state. Everyone was dependent on the government, much like on an Indian reservation. The results were similar as well. The divorce rate was high, alcoholism and drug abuse were rampant, and the people were despondent. All this began to change when the federal government, hoping to jump-start the economy of the islands, made them into a tax-free, labor-restricted zone. This meant that there was greater economic freedom in the Mariana Islands than there was in Houston. It didn't hurt that the government of the new Commonwealth of the Northern Mariana Islands was Republican.

The leaders soon hooked up with garment makers from Asia, who hired the people of the Marianas to run their factories. Eventually the citizens of the commonwealth became so prosperous that there weren't enough laborers for the factory jobs. Asians were brought in to fill these jobs, and this is when liberals on the American mainland began to worry that there was two much freedom in the middle of the Pacific Ocean.

Now freedom brings problems, and the Marianas' version of freedom was no exception. There was astonishing prosperity, but there were also the occasional charges of corruption or mistreatment of workers. Were there sweatshops? I imagine there were for a time. Were any workers ever mistreated? I can't imagine that thousands of human beings worked together without some abuses occurring. Was there prostitution or sexual slavery? Well, in 1998, I decided to investigate for myself. The Marianas government invited me to visit, because they were hoping I would help them oppose the Clinton administration's efforts to restrict the freedoms—such as being tax-free and labor union–free—that had led to astonishing prosperity in the islands.

What I found was what I said at the time: The Marianas were the Galápagos Islands of free enterprise. Amazing things were happening economically and culturally. Still, I wanted to see if there were abuses. Congressman George Miller from California had been making noise about the Marianas in Washington, and to hear him you would think thousands were trudging about in chains. I suspected that he simply didn't like the idea that the islands were free of unions and paid no taxes. This was enough to outrage a liberal. As I toured the islands I saw beautiful, air-conditioned dormitories and factories. I also saw some unfinished buildings with nasty toilets and exposed wiring that had been photographed and presented in the States as typical of conditions there. It wasn't true. I also interviewed a Catholic priest who had claimed that women were abused. He couldn't prove a single case. I even interviewed a woman who said she had had to become a stripper and a prostitute to survive. I believed her, and had compassion for her, but I didn't find her story typical. A free market means that not everyone prospers at the same rate, and people have freedom to be immoral. This may be the underside of a free market, but it is no reason to back away from the best engine of human advancement known to history.

One of my most unforgettable memories from the trip was the conduct of an ABC film crew. I had noticed they were following us, and I suspected they intended something less than the truth in their story. I became certain of this while I was attending a reception, and I looked up to see the ABC crew filming us from behind some bushes. I called to them to join us, and I said that there was no need to hide in the bushes, because we were happy to speak directly to them. They refused, and I am sure the television audience back home was later treated to scenes that were described as some secret, shady meeting attended by Tom DeLay. Pictures of me eating cheese and crackers were all they had, but they were probably more dramatic shot through tropical undergrowth.

So I did champion economic freedom for the Marianas, as I have championed economic freedom for every nation on earth. The free market, coupled with private property, small government, low taxes, and family values, will liberate a people every time. Are there challenges and abuses? Yes, but better that they result from abuses of freedom than excesses of state tyranny.

Lie Number 5: Tom DeLay gathered around him a group of corrupt characters, most of whom are now in jail.

Let's cut to the chase. I had a friendship with Jack Abramoff. We were not close, but we did like each other, and we did work together on a number of political ventures. I had known of him since his days heading the Young Republicans, and I liked him because he was a passionate conservative, a hard worker, and a gifted organizer. I also liked him, I am happy to admit, because he is an Orthodox Jew, and I have a deep love for the Jewish people. Part of this comes from my reading of the Bible, which tells me to bless and honor the Jews as God's people, and part of this is my love for the nation of Israel as a valiant beacon of democracy in the Middle East.

Jack rose to become one of the most influential lobbyists in Washington, and he was always kind to me. He supported me throughout my career, spoke well of me wherever he went, and gave me good advice on a few occasions. He never asked me to do anything unethical, never brokered our relationship so far as I knew, and never involved me in anything that was shady.

I have not seen him for years as I write this, but I understand that he has admitted to unethical and illegal behavior, and that he will serve time in jail. I've read that he apparently told the press that I had no involvement in what he is in trouble for. I'm truly sorry for him, and I trust that our God will restore him in due season. In the range of our interactions he was a good and honorable man whom I am glad I knew. That's the truth, and nothing can change it.

Another friend who has fallen into trouble is Tony Rudy. If I understand correctly, Tony has admitted to accepting money through his wife for work on a certain policy issue while he was on my staff. I hope this isn't true, but if it is I'm very disappointed in him. I still have a hard time believing it. Tony was truly like a son to me. He was a committed conservative, a brilliant staff member, and a great mind. It was thrilling to watch him struggle his way to a meaningful Christian life, and I hope that that life is a comfort to him now. As in so many cases, I knew Tony Rudy the brilliant staffer. I did not know Tony Rudy the man who has admitted to a crime.

According to press reports my dear friend Ed Buckham has also fallen under suspicion, and this deeply saddens me. Ed was like a brother to me. In fact, he was often very much like my pastor, always praying with me, encouraging me in the dark hours, and helping me take the broader view. He literally saved my career when he engineered my chairmanship of the Republican Study Committee after I had run the campaign against Newt. I might have languished on the back bench for years, but he became my champion. Ed was with me every step of the way in my leadership climb, and was my closest confidant. I owe him a huge debt. I'm praying he emerges from this season with grace and rises to be a man of righteous impact again.

Michael Scanlon was my communications director for a number of years before he went to work as a lobbyist, and later teamed with Jack Abramoff. As with the others, I knew him as a gifted strategist and a man devoted to conservative causes. Whatever character flaws or decisions may have ensnared him later were not a part of our relationship. I trust God will meet him where he is and move him on to fulfill a noble purpose.

The fact is that the vast majority of the hundreds of people who have worked for me over the years are solid people of character who served well and moved on to other roles in life. A few have come to national attention for scandal. I cannot pass judgment as to their guilt. I can say that I had no unethical or illegal involvement with any of them, and that as friends, associates, and staff members they were good people. Having been wrongly accused myself, though, I am slow to pass judgment on any man. I have learned only to pray that God grants mercy to us all.

Lie Number 6: Tom DeLay hired his wife and daughter to do nothing—
except party in Las Vegas.

I'll answer this one, but let's keep our eyes on the ball: Liberals
only go after your family because they can't beat you on the ideas. That
I have to address these charges doesn't embarrass me at all, but it is a
shameful sign of liberalism's intellectual and moral bankruptcy.

My daughter, Dani, was a public school teacher for a year after college, but she hated it. She endured all of the troubles that now plague
the public schools, and she found little backing from the administration. She grew weary of parents' expecting her to raise their children
and teach them math, too. Finally, she got fed up and left teaching.

During the summer after she resigned I needed some campaign
help. I was having trouble with my campaign manager and needed to
make a change. One day Christine was discussing some problems of our
campaign management with Ed Buckham, then our chief of staff, and
he said, "We need someone we can trust who has Tom's best interest at
heart and who is honest. Dani fits all that . . . we can teach her the rest."
When we approached Dani she resisted at first, because she had the
same aversion to politics as many kids who grow up in the homes of
politicians. She soon gave in, though, and came to work for me. She had
to intern in my Washington office for a month, and go through two different campaign management training programs. She learned fast, loved
it, and became one of the best campaign managers I've ever seen.

I'm almost embarrassed to say that I paid her twenty-five thousand
dollars a year at first, the same salary she had been making as a teacher.
This was a fraction of what she was worth. Once she learned how to run
campaigns, she was easily worth two hundred thousand dollars a year.
What she did earn from the campaign over the next ten years was easily
within acceptable range for the work she was doing. It was perfectly
legal, and worth every dime. Now what is often reported in the press is

that DeLay paid his daughter a half million bucks for no work. The truth is that she worked harder than she had in her entire life, and she did earn about half a million dollars—but over ten years, and at an average of about fifty thousand dollars a year.

The story with Christine is just about the same, but the numbers are smaller. Ed Buckham had left his chief of staff position with me and was running a PAC I had started called Americans for a Republican Majority Political Action Committee (ARMPAC). Eventually he chose to leave and start his own business. I asked Christine to help me run ARMPAC as a partnership. The ARMPAC offices were some distance away from my congressional offices, and I needed someone to keep an eye on the staff. I had been stung by mismanagement before. I could think of no one I trusted more than Christine, and her political instincts are amazing. So, the PAC hired her and paid her thirty thousand dollars a year. She was worth ten times the amount, since she was involved with all facets of the PAC, including accounting, staff, and mailings. She was the ultimate decision maker in the PAC, and her wisdom and many hours on the job not only let me give my attention to other matters, but it took ARMPAC to new heights. Liberals have charged that Christine had a "no-show" job. This is a lie. She put in many more hours than she was paid for and helped make ARMPAC truly successful. This, of course, is why the liberals raise these lies in the first place.

My hiring of Christine and Dani is indicative of a truth we need to finally accept in America. If we send good men and women to Congress their spouses and children are likely to be intelligent, hardworking people of the kind anyone would be eager to hire. This means that the people in Congress themselves would very likely wish to hire their own family members, too. As long as they aren't cooking the books and hiring family members for doing no work at all, we should let people in Congress hire their family members if that is their choice. It can mean a number of good things. It will involve family in the congressman's work, closing the destructive gap between work and home. It will also help create a cleaner moral environment in which affairs and inappropriate behavior are kept in check.

Having said this, I need to answer the lies about Dani and Las Vegas. We were attending a fund-raiser connected to ARMPAC, and Dani was along because she was the event coordinator. I was given a lovely room at the Rio Hotel, complete with a hot tub on the balcony. Now I have to say that I hate Las Vegas. Sin City isn't for me. In fact, this particular trip was the first time I had ever been to Vegas, and I've seldom gone back. So I spoke, spent the night, and flew out the next day. My room, however, had already been paid for for the second night, so I told Dani she could stay in it. That evening she invited some friends in; they partied, enjoyed the hot tub, and called it a night. Later the press began circulating reports that there had been a wild party that involved lobbyists pouring champagne on Dani in the hot tub. I asked Dani about it, and she said that the only lobbyist among the forty people at the party did pour one glass of champagne on her as a joke. I gave her some fatherly words of warning that are nobody's business, and that was the end of it. But the myth of Dani DeLay as a party girl, and of Tom DeLay arranging an orgy for lobbyists with his own daughter, has been kept alive for political gain ever since.

But then that is the point, isn't it? If we are talking about hot tubs and champagne, we aren't talking about the emptiness of liberalism. Perhaps it is time for the American people to insist on a more elevated level of political dialogue.

Lie Number 7: Tom DeLay's nickname is "The Hammer" because he frequently bullied his fellow congressmen to vote his way.

When liberals start talking about bullying in Congress, there is one name that ought to be mentioned immediately: Democrat Jim Wright. Listen to what John Murtha, a member of Wright's own party, said: Tip O'Neill "told you what he wanted done the first of the year, and never interfered with how you got it done. Jim Wright, on the other hand, not only told you what he wanted you to do, he told you how he wanted you to do it. Jim didn't get along as well."

Dick Cheney had slightly stronger words for the man: At the time he called Wright "a heavy-handed son of a bitch" and said, "he will do anything he can to win at any price, including ignoring the rules, bending rules, writing rules, denying the House the opportunity to work its will. It brings disrespect to the House itself. There's no sense of comity left."

Cheney wasn't exaggerating. Wright once guided a Democrat-run committee through a process in which a bill that had not been written yet got approved. As Congressman Don Sundquist of Tennessee complained, "Not only did they not consult with us, we had no paperwork. They approved a bill that they described to us but hadn't even written!" Now that's bullying!

Here is the bottom line: You can't bully a congressman. This may work on one vote, or maybe two, but in time resentment builds up, and the congressman becomes your enemy. The art of winning a vote is the art of persuasion and trust. It is the careful process of finding out what pressures a congressman is feeling, what will make his district happy, and how his conflicts with a bill can be resolved. You can't beat a member of Congress into submission. You win him by helping him win. I've always believed that politics is the art of the possible. If you think this way you create "win/win" situations with every vote. You must "grow the vote" by developing a relationship of trust with each member.

It is odd, by the way, that I get criticism for giving my fellow congressmen the "wine and dine" treatment, and then I get criticism for "hammering" them according to my will. My critics need to get together and get their story straight. The fact is that politics is the art of under-standing people's needs and meeting them. That's how you win a vote. That's how you win elections. That's how you offer people hope.

As for the "Hammer" nickname—which the *Washington Post* gave me as an intended insult—I like what Congresswoman Marsha Black-burn said when I left Congress: "There are two sides to a hammer. One is for hitting hard and driving nails to build something. But the other is for pulling nails when you've changed your mind, when you have a bet-ter idea and you want to start again. Tom DeLay builds fiercely, but he is always eager for new ideas and new ways to build what he dreams." In that sense, yes, I am The Hammer.

Lie Number 8: Tom DeLay illegally laundered money to fund political campaigns in Texas.

I believe it was Adolf Hitler who first acknowledged that the big lie is more effective than the little lie, because the big lie is so auda-cious, such an astonishing immorality, that people have a hard time believing anyone would say it if it wasn't true. You know, the big lie—like the Holocaust never happened or dark-skinned people are less in-telligent than light-skinned people. Well, by charging this big lie about money laundering, liberals have finally joined the ranks of scoundrels like Hitler.

Let's set the record straight. In 2001 I started a political action com-mittee, a PAC, called Texans for a Republican Majority (TRMPAC). It was designed to raise funds to support Republican candidates in Texas and around the country, and it was very successful, raising many mil-lions of dollars for conservative causes. I helped to start TRMPAC, but I was not one of its officers, I had no fiduciary responsibility for it, and I had no authority to direct its affairs.

Now Texas has a law on the books that forbids corporate money from

being used in political campaigns. Actually, administrative costs for political organizations can be paid with corporate contributions, but not the
costs of political activities. In the 2002 election year TRMPAC sent
$190,000 to the Republican National Committee that came from corpo-
rate contributors in Texas and was intended for use in states where corporate contributions are legal for political causes. In a completely separate
action the Republican National Committee sent more than $3 million—
raised from individuals in other states—into Republican campaigns in
Texas. Corporate money raised by TRMPAC and sent to the RNC never
found its way back into Texas. By the way, the Democratic National Committee did exactly the same thing in the same year with $75,000. What
they did was legal, just as what TRMPAC and the RNC did was legal.

Everything would have been fine, except for a man named Ronnie
Earle. He is the Democratic district attorney in Travis County, which
includes Austin, the capital of Texas. Earle has a reputation for filing
charges against conservative politicians—both Democrats and Republicans—until their reputations and careers are damaged, and then drop-
ping the cases before he has to prove his claims in court. In at least one
instance—that of Senator Kay Bailey Hutchinson—Earle's case actually
came to trial. He dogged Senator Hutchinson for months but the charges
just wouldn't stick, and finally the case was dropped. His tactics were a
travesty of justice. Frustrated by his lack of evidence, he even raided
Kay's offices but still did not find enough evidence to make a case. Using
the same tactics he charged me with money laundering in 2005.

It did not seem to matter to this rogue DA that there was no money-
laundering statute associated with Texas campaign finance law during
the time in question. "Money laundering" is what you do when you take
illegal money and make it clean. It happens when a man sells cocaine
and then runs his illegal money through a legal restaurant or auto parts
business, for example, to "launder," or clean up, his "dirty" money. Now

at no time was any of the money in TRMPAC or the RNC dirty. It was raised legally, and let's not forget that I had no role whatsoever in either organization other than helping them occasionally with completely legal fund-raising. That doesn't matter to Ronnie Earle. It seems to me that his only goals are media attention and character assassination. In fact, his case is so flimsy that he went through six grand juries before he found one that would indict me on laws that didn't even exist in Texas.

What Earle knew was that by indicting me on money laundering he could remove me from leadership in the Republican Party. He could do this by triggering an internal Republican rule that requires any member of the Republican leadership who is indicted for a crime to step aside. The Democratic caucus has no such rule. Ronnie Earle knew that if only he could indict me, he could remove me. So he did, and he has dragged the process along ever since, refusing to actually put his case into a courtroom where he will, frankly, get his ass kicked. He must be a political hack doing the bidding of his liberal lords in Washington, or he would show confidence in his evidence and get the case into court as fast as possible. Unfortunately, the courtroom is the last place Ronnie Earle wants to try this case. What we are witnessing is the criminalization of politics.

We are also witnessing political payback. The truth is that Democrats in Texas are trying to punish me for my role in passing a redistricting plan in 2003. That redistricting was actually a needed correction of an unfair plan the Democrats had put in place when they were the majority in Texas. However, since liberals hate the very same fairness they extol in their speeches, the Texas Democrats became so enraged by the plan that when it came time to put it to a vote, many of them fled over the state line to Oklahoma in protest. The whole nation watched in disgust as Texas governor Rick Perry was forced to dispatch state troopers in an attempt to find the fugitives.

Now I had made the claim that Democrats had unjustly redistricted in Texas long before our plan was even proposed. Let me allow an impartial source to make this case for me. The following is a quote from the *2002 Almanac of American Politics.* Listen to what it says about the Democrats' plan.

Texas's current congressional districting plan was the shrewdest gerrymander of the 1990s. . . . The plan carefully constructs Democratic districts with incredibly convoluted lines and packs heavily Republican suburban areas into just a few districts. Starting in 1994, Republicans outpolled Democrats in House races, but Democrats still have a 17-13 majority in the delegation.

Clearly there was an unfair imbalance worked into the Democrats' plan. By the election of 2001 Republicans held every statewide office in Texas but were still the minority in the House because of the injustice of the Democrats' plan.

Redistricting is an important process. The Constitution requires that redistricting occur every ten years, based upon the updated data acquired through a census. I strongly believe that this should be the job of state legislatures and not courts. I believe this because only by determining redistricting through a political process can you guarantee the right representation in a legislative body. This was the intent and genius of the Founding Fathers, but these days the process has, unfortunately, fallen into the hands of the courts, where a nonpolitical, often ideologically driven agenda guides the design of the districts.

The facts show that we brought fairness to Texas districting. In 2002, before the districts were redrawn, Democrats won 17 of the 32 seats, even though a majority of Texas voted Republican. In 2004, after our redistricting plan was put in place, about 60 percent of Texans voted Republican, and Republicans won 21 of 32 congressional seats. In other words, we fixed the Democrats' imbalance and let the will of the people prevail.

Obviously, Texas Democrats weren't happy about the change. One of the least happy was former Democratic congressman Martin Frost. He lost his seat during the redistricting I helped engineer in 2003, and has had a vendetta against me ever since. He started a PAC called Lone Star Fund that not only opposed almost everything I was for in Texas, but has also been credited with funding many of the Democratic victories in the 2006 election. I'm convinced that Ronnie Earle and Martin Frost are conspiring together. Unable to defeat us in the House, and unwilling to engage in the difficult battle for the minds and hearts of the American people, Democrats like these simply went after Republican leaders like me at the most vicious and personal level. Thus, Ronnie Earle's tactics, thus charges based on no existing law, and thus the unceasing bombardment of Tom DeLay's world.

Lie Number 9: Tom DeLay cynically "got religion" so he could ride the rising wave of the religious right in the 1980s.

I am not offended by this suspicion. I know that politicians often use religion to win votes, and I'm not surprised that people think I might have done the same. I didn't. The truth is that in 1985 I had a genuine born-again experience. Jesus Christ took up residence in my life, healed my marriage, changed my passions, and gave me a new map for understanding the world. Twenty-two years later I think the verdict is in: Tom DeLay is not perfect, but he is a sincere Christian.

What my critics may not realize, though, is that my faith has cost me as much politically as it has gained me, perhaps even more. Consider:

• I chose to call for Bill Clinton's resignation and then pursue his impeachment because my faith leads me to believe that a president must set an example to the nation morally and legally. Voters did not agree, and in the next election after impeachment we Republicans found ourselves in the fight of our lives. We actually lost seats in the House over it. I did what my faith inspired me to do, but it wasn't the safest move politically.

- My Bible teaches me that I should bless and support the nation of Israel. I have done so repeatedly, and will until my dying day. I can tell you, though, that when Israeli shells are falling in Palestinian territory supporting Israel is one of the most costly stands an American politician can take. My faith guides me, though, and I will always support a strong, stable Israel.

- My faith teaches me that life is sacred because human beings are made in the image of God. I believe that the unborn should not be killed because they are unwanted, and the brain-damaged should not be killed because they are not "normal." This is what moved me to call for the intervention of Congress in the Terri Schiavo case. It was the right thing to do, and I wish we had been successful, but it was politically damaging. I have been vilified nationwide for trying to stop Terri's murder, and the criticism continues to this day. Still, my faith compelled me.

My point is that my devotion to Jesus Christ and the Bible has not guaranteed an easy path in politics. Quite the contrary. Nevertheless, on these matters of faith and a dozen others like them, I can offer no apology, no retreat, and no surrender. Like Martin Luther, "Here I stand." I am a Christian. I can do no other.

Lie Number 10: Tom DeLay left office because he is guilty of crimes and he is trying to avoid prosecution.

In an environment of accusation and suspicion even righteous actions are treated with suspicion. This describes perfectly the response I received when I chose to leave Congress. I made the decision for what I believe are noble reasons, but there continue to be suspicions and pet theories that put my choice in the most negative light. I'm glad for the chance to finally face down the lies with the truth.

I left Congress after four to five weeks of prayer. I can't remember ever wanting to know the will of God quite like I did during that season. It was a tumultuous time, and I did not want to make my decision out of anger, fear, or cowardice. Ronnie Earle's indictment had been handed down, and I had to leave my post as majority leader because of the internal Republican party rule preventing an indicted congressman from serving in leadership.

As I mentioned earlier, Democrats had no such rule about indicted congressmen serving in leadership. That was a rule Newt Gingrich, Dick Armey, and I had pushed for when Republicans took over Congress in 1994. The Democrats tried to win control of the Congress back from us in the five subsequent elections, and failed each time. So they did what they do best: They used our own rules against us and made sure I was indicted. (You've probably heard the saying that indictments are handed down so easily even a ham sandwich could be indicted.)

Some of my friends who were members of the Texas delegation saw this bogus indictment coming down the pike, and urged the rest of the House Republicans to amend the rule before it took me out (and the Republican majority with it). They suggested that if an indictment were proven to be politically motivated—as mine certainly was—the rule could be waived on a case-by-case basis. Denny Hastert thought this made sense, and so the rule was amended by the conference.

As you might imagine, the media had a field day with that development. Newt Gingrich and Dick Armey, who were no longer serving in Congress, roundly criticized the amendment in a very public way. The preexisting tensions I had with Gingrich and Armey partially explain why they said what they said about me in the press.

Denny Hastert heeded the criticism, and led the Republican conference to reverse course. I guess he did what he felt he had to do, but I disagreed with it. Of course the perception was that if even Hastert was against me, I must have done something truly wrong. The torrent of vicious attacks gained force. My family and I were enduring character assassination of a type that I had rarely seen in Washington.

In the middle of the storm I could still be practical. Though I had won my primary by a sizable margin, I knew I had only a 50–50 chance of being reelected given the public attacks I had endured. I also knew that even if elected, I would be relegated to the back bench. I thought it might be best to let someone else run for my seat. In addition, I did not want to be a burden around the necks of other Republican candidates in the country, who were likely to have the lies about Tom DeLay lobbed at them during the heat of a campaign.

Perhaps as important, after twenty-two years in Congress I yearned to be free of the restraints of office to advance conservative causes and support Israel. The constant press of a congressman's schedule and the exhausting business of fending off the politics of personal destruction had made me hunger for a simpler, more streamlined, more effective life. I found myself dreaming of what I might do outside of Congress to support the values I had championed for nearly forty years. I wanted more than an elder statesman's role, though. I wanted to shape the thinking of my generation and the politics of our nation for a generation after that.

All of this led me to the decision to resign. I consulted with Bill Paxon, my pastor, and a few close supporters. They were immensely helpful but ultimately the decision was mine, and I made it: It was time for me to go. Once it was settled in my soul, I felt free.

People have often commented about the smile on my face in the "mug shot" that the police took when I was indicted. I wish I could tell you that I felt nothing but peace. It wouldn't be true, though. It was very humiliating to walk through that jail—hearing the doors clang behind me, having insults yelled at me by convicts in orange uniforms, and being slammed up against a wall to have my picture taken. My lawyer had told me to smile for the camera, but I didn't think I could. I said a prayer, though, and offered the best smile I could muster. All I wanted was for people to see Jesus in my life at that horrible moment. Thankfully, the picture my enemies wanted so desperately to be a sign of my downfall became instead a symbol of my new life. And believe me, that new life has just begun!

AMERICAN DREAMS

Newt Gingrich tells a story of escorting two *Pravda* reporters around Washington. *Pravda*, of course, was the leading newspaper of the old Soviet Union and an arm of the Communist Party. After showing these men the monuments of the city, Newt took them to the empty House of Representatives, where one of the reporters asked if he could stand behind the rostrum. The man walked slowly up the steps, looked out for a moment upon the great hall, and then gently slid into the speaker's chair. When he walked down to rejoin Newt and the other reporter he said solemnly, "Now I have sat at the center of freedom."

It is often overlooked today that the Founding Fathers intended Congress to be the chief political institution of our land. While presidents are easier to focus on in our media age, and the Supreme Court makes the occasional high-profile ruling, the nation's business is conducted in Congress, as it should be. In fact, though the decisions of presidents are often treated by the press as the mandates of monarchs, the truth is that presidents get very little done without Congress. This is more true of the House of Representatives than it is of the Senate. Since all tax matters and appropriations of funds arise in the House, presidents can get little done without its cooperation. As politically astute as Ronald Reagan was, he got only about 25 percent of what he wanted because the Democratic-controlled House was not with him. The first president Bush only got about 10 percent of what he wanted, and the Democratic House manipulated him into breaking his pledge to not raise taxes. For six years Bill Clinton got virtually nothing he wanted because of the Republican House. In short, the House is where the governing action is, though the media action may be elsewhere.

As I write these words it is a few months after the midterm elections of 2006, and already the press is filled with predictions of who will be president in 2008. Comparisons of Hillary Clinton to Barack Obama, and of John McCain to Rudolph Giuliani, abound. Already there are polls about which spouse will make the best First Lady—or First Man— and the nation seems ready to skip the next two years in its political life and move directly to a presidential vote. Part of this, of course, is wishful thinking: The vast majority of Americans are dissatisfied with George W. Bush and eager for a change. A great deal of this anticipation, though, is due to the media appeal of a presidential race and a general ignorance of how powerful Congress truly is.

In the next few years our government is going to make some of the most important decisions in American history. The simple truth is that we are at a turning point in our nation, and our approach to issues like the war on terror, immigration, taxation, the role of religion in our national life, abortion, and the rule of law rather than the rule of judges in our courts will determine whether the vision of the Founding Fathers is to be fulfilled, or whether a far removed vision is put in place instead. If what I say is true, then the battle for Congress will become the battle for the nation's destiny.

This is why I regard the Republican loss of the House and the Senate in 2006 as a grand opportunity. It is a wake-up call, a summons to battle. Democrats did not win that election; Republicans lost it. And if

Republicans will seriously examine why they lost, and reclaim what had given them victory in the first place, they will arise, I believe, to rescue this nation in the coming decades.

The polls show that Republicans lost the election over frustration with Bush, the war, and a general perception of Republican incompetence and lack of principles. I would suggest that Republicans lost because they did not communicate their message and their victories with enough strength to overcome short-term, media-fed issues that arose right before the election. Republicans were, as they long have been, right on the issues and terrible at communication. There are few articulate spokesmen among the current Republican or conservative leadership, and this is a huge disadvantage.

Consider, for example, the Mark Foley scandal. I knew Mark Foley as a rather mediocre, undisciplined, and ineffective congressman. He was a party boy. I did not know he was gay, but it would not have mattered. In Congress you work with whomever the people send, and the people of Florida chose to send a gay congressman. Though I believe homosexuality is a perverse lifestyle and a sin before God, I have worked with a number of gay congressmen—like Jim Kolbe, known for attending official functions with his male lover—who were competent and effective. Foley was not among them and, though I knew nothing about his flirtations with congressional pages, I was not surprised at his conduct.

Unfortunately, when the story broke, Denny Hastert came in for a media bashing because he had been given some light warnings about Foley several years earlier. The truth was that no one among the Republican leadership had had any idea what Foley was really up to, because he had lied repeatedly, telling the leadership that he had stopped any questionable activity. Yet when the facts came out they revealed that Foley had devoted most of his efforts to pursuing a nineteen-year-old former page. This was not only a legal relationship but one that Denny Hastert had no authority to question. The problem was that the Republican communication apparatus is so poor that people still think there was some kind of cover-up of Foley's activities by the Republican leadership. This is completely untrue, but who could the nation look to among Republicans for clear, visionary, passionate articulation of their views?

Then, of course, there was the war. By the time of the election Americans were weary of the war and thought the Democrats could make a change. They will find, in time, that their confidence was misplaced, yet the larger issue for Republicans is how they lost the media battle over a war that every Democrat voted for, that the nation endorsed from its beginning, and which has become difficult only as all wars do for a season. God knows if the same brand of media coverage had been present during the American revolution and World War II we would now be Englishmen sixty years into a Nazi occupation.

Not long ago I was on Fox News's hit talk show *Hannity and Colmes* and Sean Hannity showed clips from his interviews during a trip to Iraq with American soldiers and Marines. It was almost overwhelming to hear from the lips of these fighting men and women what we almost never hear from the press. They told of how they believe in their fight, of how the Iraqis want them to stay, of what the stakes really are, and of how the war could be won if there was greater support in Washington. I told Sean that he had to get these interviews out to the nation, because they tell a different story than the distortions that have become the American media diet. I even called Tony Snow, the White House press secretary, and urged him to let the soldiers answer the critics of the war. I knew that if the average American could hear the truth from those risking all to fight this war they would understand why Republicans have stood so firmly for a decisive victory.

I have long believed that George W. Bush has neglected his greatest weapon in convincing Americans about the war: the fighting men and women

NO RETREAT, NO SURRENDER

themselves. Franklin Roosevelt used to bring valiant soldiers from the front and put them before the American people. In this way the folks at home could hear the truth and be inspired by those on the battle lines. It worked. America has seldom been as unified as it was during World War II. I believe it could be again. I've urged the Bush administration to put the soldiers and Marines front and center in the culture war over Iraq. Typically, though, no one at the Bush White House is listening.

I should say here that I completely supported Donald Rumsfeld's approach to the war when he was secretary of defense. He has been a close friend and adviser to me for twenty years, and I have deep respect for him. I also believe that his leadership was wise and his strategies were effective while he was in office. This doesn't mean that mistakes weren't made. They were. But mistakes will always be made on battlefields. Wars are barely controlled chaos, and failure is not defined by having problems; it is defined by having problems that you don't address aggressively. Don Rumsfeld addressed problems in a courageous manner and the country was lucky to have him in office, as was Bush, whether he knew it or not.

I should also say here that I am completely opposed to the recommendations of the Iraq Study Group. They should change their name to the Iraq Surrender Group. The simple truth is that if we are going to win the war on terror worldwide, we are going to have to win the war in Iraq. Our failures have not been on the battlefield. They have been in not winning the minds and the hearts of the American people. We have allowed people to sit in the comfort of their homes and not feel the sense of threat that Islamic terrorism represents in the world. This leads them to believe that the war is optional, that it is something our leaders jumped into without cause. This is both false and foolish. We needed to win the people in order to win the war, but we did not.

The critical point is that once again Republicans are doing the right thing but are letting the spin masters convince America otherwise. This is central to the Republican crisis. Because most Republicans are businessmen who go to Washington to limit government rather than expand it, and because Republicans tend to be doers rather than just performers, they don't tend to see themselves as media figures. What some have called "the vision thing"—the ability to paint a grand and mobilizing vision for the American people—does not come naturally to them. The result is that liberal lies fill the vacuum of Republican silence. I consider George W. Bush, Dick Cheney, and Denny Hastert all to be good men, but there is not an articulate voice among them. Though I certainly put myself in that same inarticulate category, it doesn't change the reality that we need conservative Churchills in the years to come, men and women able to speak of both facts and values with poetry and force.

Because we did not have the apparatus of skilled communication in place, we lost a critical election, and did so during a Republican Congress that served the nation magnificently. Just think of what they brought us. They fought the war on terror, set the rules for trying terrorists in military tribunals, reformed the Patriot Act, strengthened homeland security, and resolved the wiretapping issue. They extended tax cuts, sent three bills to the president addressing tort reform, lowered the deficit, lowered government spending, passed a comprehensive energy plan, and reformed the appropriations committee. This is nowhere near the complete list, and yet the Republicans who led this wonderfully successful Congress were removed from office largely by Americans who believed that they had failed. Clearly the Republicans failed to make their victories known and their values clear.

Fortunately, there is still time to rise. The election of 2006 didn't signal a massive philosophical change among the American people. They were simply reacting to Bush and the war. Americans are still a largely conservative lot who want constitutional government, strong defense, protected borders, low taxes, honor for their American heritage, and traditional family values. This is what the Republicans stand for. If the party will play to win, build the machinery necessary for victory, focus on Churchillian communication, and refuse to do a Bush-like compromise of its core conservative values, Republicans can win.

The stakes are too high for the Republicans to miss this opportunity. Liberal ideas are dying. What you hear is the death rattle of an outworn and misguided worldview. Most thinking people understand that big government, high taxes, a managed economy, weak defense, an activist judiciary, a low regard for the law, a low regard for American values and traditions, and a refusal to both protect our nation from invasion at its border and to pass our distinctive values on to the next generation will mean the death of America. The future belongs to those who hold to time-honored values, who get government off the backs of the people, who liberate creativity in a free market, who uphold the rule of law, who insist on American exceptionalism, who protect that exceptionalism with a strong defense and impregnable borders, and who live to fashion a world of freedom and prosperity for the next generation. In my view history will view the Republican revolution as merely the great rehearsal for a glorious American age, and conservatives must prepare to fashion that age if it is ever to become a reality.

This preparation must begin with understanding the nature of our fight. The truth is that Republicans are now facing a well-financed, highly organized coalition of liberal organizations, including the media, that is devoted to long-range victory for the political left. This was evident in the last election, an election in which liberals were victorious without ideas or alternatives but simply on the strength of their well-financed coalition. The evolution of this network can be tracked to the last days of the Clinton administration. Many of Clinton's former staffers—whom I call "Clintonistas"—formed themselves into a network—which I call the "liberal mafia"—devoted to winning House and Senate races. Their sophistication is impressive. Their funding is staggering. Their connections are awesome. The painful truth is that conservatives have nothing like it.

To understand this coalition further, log onto www.discoverthenetwork.org. My friend David Horowitz has done a marvelous job of mapping the liberal mafia and making both its power and its intentions known. The bottom line is that when Hillary Clinton complained of a "vast right-wing conspiracy," there wasn't one. There is, however, a vast left-wing conspiracy today, and Republicans urgently need to awaken to its potential if they are going to reclaim their former heights.

Republicans also need to reclaim a clear agenda if they are going to rise again. I believe there is a simple, five-point agenda that should guide our efforts in the days to come. I offer it here as a rallying cry to conservatives. We *must* come together and fight for our first principles.

First, we must win the war on terror. This will mean shaking off the disillusionment and moral stagnation that currently besets us and assuring the security any nation needs to achieve greatness. To accomplish this we will have to aggressively pursue international terrorism, secure our borders, and be willing to punish insurgents severely at home and abroad.

Second, we must have fundamental tax reform. We desperately need a fair tax in this country, one that eliminates all federal taxes and replaces them with one sales tax. The resulting revenues will determine how much the nation will pay for its federal government. The people should not be forced to pay more than 10 percent of their income to support their government.

Third, we must redefine government. It is time for a return to our constitutional system. The federal government is currently failing the

people because it attempts to do what the Constitution never gave it the authority to do. We must downsize government as a whole, returning it to constitutional boundaries. The Departments of Education, Commerce, and Energy should be abolished; the Department of Agriculture should be severely downsized; and the Department of Homeland Security should be dramatically restructured. Ultimately, Congress must be reformed and restored to its ascendancy in our constitutional system.

Fourth, we must hold the judiciary accountable and fight judicial activism. A brief survey of early American political theory will show that the Founding Fathers never intended the judiciary to hold the power it does today. Now activist judges usurp the will of the people and do untold damage through decisions based more on radical ideologies than on the law of the land. The Constitution gives power to Congress to restrict the judiciary, and it is time for a grand correction to the judicial excess of our time.

Fifth, we must fight and win the culture war. We conservatives can no longer divide ourselves into fiscal conservative and cultural conservative camps. Our beliefs must flow into every area of life. We must stand for a comprehensive world and life view. It is time to protect the family, end abortion, defend traditional marriage, insist upon moral values in the public schools, and empower individuals and private organizations to address the nation's social ills. Conservatism is not just a political platform. It is a lens of faith, heritage, wisdom, and character through which we learn to see the world. It is time for that lens to be offered to our generation.

This is the five-point platform that I believe Republicans should execute in the years to come. We should accomplish these goals at the same time that we develop a counter to the vast liberal network that we now face. The moment has come to rebuild the conservative movement.

We have proven the truth of our ideas. Now we must build the network of organizations that will embed those ideas permanently into the American future. Liberalism has no ideas, only political machinery. If we can wed our ideas to a massive vehicle of cultural and political transformation, we can restore this nation to greatness.

Yet it would be wrong to believe that the American future is bright because government will make it so. My entire political life has been devoted to forcing government back into its constitutional cage so that the American people may achieve their intended magnificence. This is why I have great hope for the future. I believe that the verdict is in, and that government has been proven an inferior engine of human advancement when compared to the private sector. All the world has seen the Republican revolution in this country and now understands that prosperity comes from conservative values. Only fools would ignore these lessons in the future. This means that the focus can shift to the individual and to people solving social ills through compassion and their God-given abilities. Who knows what may come of this? We may witness a great age of social transformation. We may see poverty wiped out, learning achieve new heights, families restored as the foundation of society, and sacrificial service become the defining ethic of our time.

Christine and I discovered the desperate need to roll back government and serve the hurting through private means when we confronted the debacle of foster care. It was Christine who first understood what was happening. She was asked to become a Court-Appointed Special Advocate (CASA). The CASA program was designed by a Washington state judge, and was intended to assure that every child brought into protective services because of abuse or neglect was assigned a trained advocate. Sadly, abuse is epidemic in foster care. It was Christine's job to get to know them, to understand their cases, and to speak for them in court if necessary. She was very passionate about the plight of the children,

and she refused to back down if she felt a child was receiving poor representation by the government or the appointed attorney. My wife being able to do nothing by halves, she threw herself into the job. She ended up on the board of Fort Bend Child Advocates and started golf tournaments to raise money for the cause. Over time she raised millions of dollars for this worthy work, and there is even a building named after us, not for my career but for her passionate service as a child advocate.

What Christine began to tell me about the plight of foster children broke my heart. I learned that the symbol of a foster child is a black garbage bag, because every time a child is moved—and with most children it is too often—they have to gather their belongings into that familiar black plastic bag. Though many people who become foster parents are caring, devoted people, some do it only for the money, and some, unfortunately, do it for more perverse reasons. Christine learned that pedophiles often worked their way into the system, and that many kids become runaways to avoid the cruelties of the very home that was meant to provide care. The worst foster care in the country is in Washington, D.C. One of my friends and a former staffer, Dr. Cassie Bevan Statuto, is a brilliant child advocate in D.C. who serves on a board that investigates the deaths of foster children. Think of it: There are so many deaths among foster children—the very lives the system is supposed to protect and care for—that they had to create a permanent board to investigate child murders.

In time I would learn about the challenges of foster care from firsthand experience, and not just from Christine's accounts. Christine was assigned to a seventeen-year-old girl in the system who was a runaway. Unfortunately, the system often doesn't respond when older kids run away, and the girls frequently end up in some of the least desirable jobs that a woman can get. This is a costly form of neglect, because a huge percentage of Texas prisoners are former foster children who might have been saved. So when Christine tracked the girl down and tried to find a

foster home for her, at least until she graduated from high school, she quickly found out that it is very difficult to find a home for a teenager. That's when Christine suggested that we become foster parents for this child. Now I don't mind admitting that my first objections were political. I was the majority whip at the time, and I didn't want my detractors to write that I was taking in a runaway for political purposes. I could see that Christine was eager to make a difference in this girl's life, so I decided we could do it if we were careful to avoid publicity. Christine agreed; we both went to the courses required of foster parents, and we became foster parents.

It was more difficult than either of us imagined. Our foster daughter resisted our every boundary and attempt to help. One morning Christine went downstairs and found a man in bed with her. We didn't give up on her, though, and we were determined not to kick her out, but it was a trial. Finally, after three months, the girl left on her own, which was her habit. Christine felt like a failure and swore that she didn't want another foster child. In six months, though, she called and asked me if we could take in another.

The problem for most foster children is that every time they leave a home they have to grieve the loss of a family as though death has taken them away. Many of these kids are nothing but scar tissue. They are usually diagnosed with attachment disorders that develop from repeatedly attaching to a family just to be jerked up and removed at a moment's notice. They have poor self-concepts because society has told them by word and deed that they are worthless. This is how we would describe our second foster daughter's condition. Determined to see better results than with the first child, Christine worked with this new daughter intently, won the battle of trust, instilled some discipline, and eventually saw a beautiful young lady graduate from high school, then college, and ultimately be happily married with a child.

We fostered one other child and so we were successful with some, less so with others. Always we were confronted by how awful the system is. We kept seeing how it was a fertile ground for abusers, and how few children turned out healthy and successful. It is a government system, after all, and government systems rarely work well in arenas like this. The truth is it doesn't take a village to raise a child. It takes a mom and a dad with love and a long-term commitment.

We began to challenge ourselves to design a different kind of system. If money was no barrier, we said, what would we do to solve the crisis of foster care in this country? Christine began studying successful homes to learn what the best practices were to help these kids become healthy, successful adults. In the meantime we had already started the DeLay Foundation for Kids for charitable work, and I began raising money through it for the budding vision. In time I did fundraisers and sought contributions from people I knew would care about the kids as we did.

Finally Christine put the finishing touches on the vision. She wanted a place where the kids had a permanent home in a community that cared about them. If the parents no longer wanted to be involved, the parents left, not the kids. Christine had learned of this from a trip to Israel. In their program the children are permanent. The parents may go but the children always have a constant home of their own. We knew our program would have to have a Christian base and a strong emphasis on sports, and to encourage a full social life. We also wanted it to be a physically beautiful place that would tell the children they were valued.

The dream has become a reality. The George Foundation gave us land in Richmond, Texas, and with the money we raised we were able to build what is best described as a subdivision. It is called the Riobend (www.riobend.org), and it is beautiful. Christine has done a marvelous job. The houses have been designed uniquely to accommodate both the family life of the foster parents and their involvement in the lives of the foster kids. The grounds are beautiful, there is a chapel at the heart of it all, and Christine works with a marvelous staff to develop what I think is becoming one of the most innovative facilities in the world.

From time to time, though, Christine hasn't been able to resist a jab at some of our critics. Once I got involved in this cause I had numerous reporters wondering aloud if the whole foster care emphasis in my life wasn't just an excuse for a "political slush fund." Christine finally wearied of it. She took to showing journalists like Chris Matthews around the facility and saying, "Welcome to Tom DeLay's political slush fund!" She never does behave.

Beyond the miraculous work Riobend does for the kids, its meaning to me has a great deal to do with what can happen in America when individuals serve others and don't assume that government will get the job done. Not only was government never designed for such functions, it does it badly when it tries, and it does it wastefully with forced taxation. The folks at Riobend have shown, as have millions of other Americans who solve social ills through private funds and systems, that people serving with compassion and their innate talents make a difference government never will.

This, then, is my dream for America. I do not dream of a Republican ascendancy. I do not dream of better government at the hands of a different party. I dream of government moving off the center stage of our society in order to free the God-given greatness of a people. This was the dream of our founders. This was the motivating dream of my political life. This is the dream that will assure the glory of America for generations yet to come.

Perhaps now you understand the title of this book. I stand resolute in my values not because I am an inherently stubborn, combative man. I stand firm because I believe conservative values are the key to American greatness. I remain unyielding about my fight in Congress, my fights in the courts, and my fight for the hearts and minds of the American people because I believe the lives of the next generation depend on it. Most of all I remain undaunted because I believe that my conservative values arise from Scripture, from the counsel of the Founding Fathers, and from the wisdom of the American experience. This is why I say, "No retreat, No surrender."

Not to liberal tyranny. Not to the politics of personal destruction. Not to the lies of the leftist political machine. I am a Christian, a conservative, and a man deeply in love with his country. This is who I am. Here is where I stand. No retreat. No surrender.

INDEX

PHOTO CREDITS